G000162176

MULTIPLES
IIIUMINATED

Life with Twins and Triplets, the Toddler to Tween Years

Edited by
Megan Woolsey and Alison Lee

MULTIPLES ILLUMINATED
Life with Twins and Triplets, the Toddler to Tween Years
Copyright © 2017 by Multiples Illuminated
ISBN 978-0-9968335-1-6

All rights reserved. No part of this publication may be reproduced, stored in a retrieval system or transmitted in any form or by any means, electronic, mechanical, photocopying, recording or otherwise, without the prior written permission of the author.

This book identifies product names and services known to be trademarks, registered trademarks, or service marks of their respective holders. They are used throughout this book in an editorial fashion only. In addition, terms suspected of being trademarks, registered trademarks, or service marks have been appropriately capitalized, although the authors cannot attest to the accuracy of this information. Use of a term in this book should not be regarded as affecting the validity of any trademark, registered trademark, or service mark.

Multiples Illuminated: Life with Twins and Triplets, the Toddler to Tween Years

Published 2017

CONTENTS

MULTIPLES IIIUMINATED

Life with Twins and Triplets, the Toddler to Tween Years

FOREWORD

JOAN A. FRIEDMAN, Ph.D

At the age of 40, I had a feeling of unfinished business, an incompleteness. I wanted one more child to round out my family: I came from a family of four siblings and wanted to have four children of my own. Already the mother of three beautiful children, ages eight, six, and four, I felt up to the challenge of having one last baby before my childbearing window closed. Even though it was 26 years ago, I vividly recall calling my husband with the news that we were going to have twins. Ever the optimist, he responded to my shock and dismay with the reassuring response, "Well, at least it's not triplets!"

My primary fear about bringing twins into the world was not the pregnancy or the birth. Rather, being an identical twin myself and having experienced some residual emotional turmoil stemming from my relationship with my sister Jane, I had all sorts of worries and anxiety about how I would raise my own twins. Since I was fortunate to have eight years of parenting under my belt already, I was not excessively worried about being anything more than a 'good enough' parent. I did not feel as if I had to prove myself to anyone or justify decisions that I made prior to the birth of my twins, Jonny and David. I came equipped with my own ideas about how I intended to raise two very individuated sons so that they would not suffer as much as Jane and I did in attempting to define and create our separate identities.

1

Not long ago, Jane shared a story with me about an incident that occurred when we were in high school. At that time, academically gifted students were given the opportunity to take an exam to determine their eligibility to take a year-long college-level course at a prestigious university. Jane qualified for the honor, and I did not. She attended the college course for only one semester. She confessed that she deliberately decided not to attend the second semester because she felt guilty that I had not qualified to do what she had achieved. I was aghast and sad to hear about the personal sacrifice she felt she had to make in order to preserve our connection.

Many parents raising twins are so conditioned by popular notions and fantasies about twins that they shy away from thinking outside the box or taking actions that might be considered by others to be wrong, dangerous, or unconscionable. However, I felt liberated and excited about embracing counterintuitive parenting approaches that might lessen the stigma imposed by the 'twin mystique.' More often than not, the non-twin world lumps twins together and sees them as 'identical'—even when they are a boy and a girl!

My husband and I decided that we would not tell anyone which boy was 'older.' As I had always been identified as the older twin by virtue of my entry into the world three minutes before Jane, I wanted my sons to be free of this burdensome label that means absolutely nothing—especially in the case of a Cesarean birth where one baby is pulled out literally seconds after the other. Also, the boys had distinct-sounding names, not alliterative ones, and they had middle names, too. Jane and I were assigned a middle initial according to our birth order (Joan A. and Jane B.) rather than being given proper middle names like our other two siblings. In addition, I made sure there were separate pictures of each of my sons, and made two baby books with shared and single photos. I took each boy out alone as much as I was able and did not introduce him as being a twin. I spent a considerable amount of time using my single stroller, getting acquainted with each twin's distinct personality and temperament.

As you can imagine, my husband and I were too overwhelmed to maintain the schedule and structure that we'd had with our three older children. On more nights than I care to admit, Jonny and David fell asleep on our bed along with our Labradors because we did not have the energy to get the boys to their room. Our older children will tell you that their brothers enjoyed a comparatively more lenient and indulgent upbringing because our parental fatigue overpowered our capacity to impose schedules and rules.

Nonetheless, Jonny and David benefited immeasurably from the love, attention, and guidance provided by their older siblings. My daughters dressed them up and played games with them, and my son—the oldest child—initiated lots of physical activities that they all enjoyed. Even though my younger daughter, who was four when she found out she was having twin brothers, superciliously instructed us to name them *Shit* and *Pooh Pooh*, she grew to love her brothers.

I must say that I enjoyed parenting Jonny and David so much for two primary reasons. First of all, not being a first-time mom freed me from some of the constraints of conformity and social acceptance. For example, my husband and I let Jonny and David's hair grow quite long because we loved their blond curls. However, this situation dramatically changed one day. We were at a friend's home swimming and the boys had no bathing suits on—they were about three years old at the time. An inquisitive four-year-old girl looked at Jonny and David and then walked over to me and asked, "How come those girls have a penis?" Their first haircut was scheduled soon after that!

The second and more salient point that contributed to my pride and satisfaction was being able to raise Jonny and David in a manner aligned with their needs and individuality.

I felt empowered and successful making decisions about the boys' lives, which on many occasions raised eyebrows and created skepticism. My husband and I were confronted innumerable times by people who were absolutely aghast at our efforts to ensure separate experiences for our twins—beginning with our decision not to tell anyone which boy was older until they turned 13, and remaining steadfastly committed to the goal that they would be prepared to attend different colleges. We worked out a developmentally appropriate timeline that would enable the boys to handle themselves without their twin. Although the boys sometimes did not enjoy themselves, we arranged for separate classes, separate sports teams, separate day camps, and separate overnight camps. The consistent message was our persistent focus to help them develop the resilience and capacity to manage on their own.

I don't want to gloss over the difficult issues that cropped up for them. They faced a number of dilemmas over their very different capacities to socialize. Jonny, being on the quieter side, had difficulty making friends, while other kids would flock to the outgoing and gregarious David. Jonny was certainly aware of this divergence. As young as seven, he voiced his resentment that everyone liked David better. David was invited to many play dates with friends that the boys did not share. It was incredibly painful to listen to Jonny's sad and resentful feelings about not being included; nonetheless, we honored David's separate experiences and organized some special times for Jonny. Of course, what Jonny could not appreciate at the time was that my husband and I recognized Jonny's distinct temperament. Jonny preferred quiet, contemplative time to build intricate and complicated structures with his set of wooden blocks. He enjoyed 'getting lost' in a creative endeavor – and still does. He does not need a large group of friends. He is content with one or two close buddies, and David.

David had to contend with a myriad of learning issues diagnosed when he entered kindergarten. So, he was not capable of accomplishing the artistic and musical successes that Jonny achieved. Moreover, David's growth lagged behind Jonny's until they turned 18. He was diagnosed with intrauterine growth retardation. He was always labeled 'the small twin.' Thankfully no intervention other than time was required. He is blessed with a personality that exudes optimism. He enjoys his work, loves being around people, and excels at finding terrific women to take care of him! Although his learning difficulties continue to present challenges, he has developed effective strategies and coping skills to manage.

These differences did not produce unmanageable competition or discord because the boys had been raised in a family culture where individuality was clearly celebrated and encouraged. The joy and satisfaction I feel watching them interact as adults are beyond expression. Jonny and David are emotionally close, temperamentally opposite, and authentically respectful and loving.

The beauty of reading this wonderful collection of stories in this second anthology of *Multiples Illuminated* is the sharing of our unique family experiences. When I speak as a 'twin expert,' I qualify my remarks by emphasizing that no parenting philosophy should espouse the notion that 'one size fits all.' How we choose to raise our children is a composite of our individual life experiences, our values and ethics, and our communities. Learning about varied ideas and approaches is the lens through which we can expand our consciousness and grow. You will thoroughly enjoy reading these terrific essays. You will laugh, cry, and smile, and feel a shared kinship with other parents of multiples navigating their lives together.

Dr. Joan A. Friedman is a gifted psychotherapist who has devoted many years of her professional career to educating twins and their families about twins' emotional needs. Having worked through her own twinship challenges and parented her fraternal twin sons, she is a definitive expert about twin development. She is the author of Emotionally Healthy Twins: A New Philosophy for Parenting Two Unique Children *and* The Same but Different: How Twins Can Live, Love, and Learn to Be Individuals.

INTRODUCTION

MEGAN WOOLSEY AND ALISON LEE

An American writer and humorist Josh Billings wrote in the 1800s, "There are two things in this life for which we are never truly prepared, and that is twins."

After Megan's initial shock of finding out she was having triplets, and surviving the first couple of years of managing three babies at once, she had to confront the reality of the next stage. A stage she had only undertaken with a singleton. How will she help the triplets with their homework each night? Will they be in the same classroom? What about play dates and after-school activities – will they be happy doing the same thing or will it be a case of prioritizing one child's activity over the other?

Alison used the opening quote above to announce her twin pregnancy to friends and family. Alongside the joy, there was also trepidation about what was to come. The toddler stage is challenging with one child – with multiples, everything is amplified. How do moms of multiples manage going out of the house with little ones now capable of running off in different directions at the same time? How do we give the right amount of attention to each child at any given time?

Megan's triplets are now nine. Alison's twins turn three in September this year. The days have been long, and the years short. With a few more wrinkles and gray hair, we have both come to appreciate how much we have learned in parenting our multiples through the years, and what they teach us every day. Other than the lessons we have learned as parents, we have also learned how much the idea of twins, triplets, or more matter in society at large.

Multiples are a fascination, not just to those who have twins, triplets, or more, or who are a twin or triplet themselves. Multiples elicit a 'wow' response, whether it be, "Wow, they are twins/triplets?" or "Wow, you have your hands full!"

The celebrity news dominating headlines earlier this year are stories and pictures of Beyoncé and Jay Z or George and Amal Clooney, pregnant with twins, along with Pharrell Williams and Helen Lasichanh, who recently welcomed triplets into their family. One popular television show, *This is Us,* revolves around multiples.

No one, however, is more fascinated or enamored with multiples, than parents and family members of twins, triplets, or more. Whether you are an experienced parent or a new one, there is nothing quite like it. Everything changes. From the logistics of travel to the complexities of tending to the needs and feelings of children at the same developmental age, no one day is the same as another. Our experiences are different from those of people raising singletons.

Another popular response to multiples is the concept of Irish Twins, pushed to you by those who have children close in age, or know people who do. "It's the same thing!"

It's hardly the same thing. The discussion arises when opposite ends of this spectrum meet. It must be more difficult with multiples, because oh my goodness, three babies crying all at once! Some mothers of multiples will tell you that it's actually more challenging to have children close in age – to be pregnant and caring for a baby or toddler is no mean feat.

These wow responses, and discussions about multiples and their families are some of the topics you'll find in this book. We want to lift the veil off the many mysteries and wonders of raising multiples, not just for families with multiples, but for those who are fascinated by it.

In 2016, we embarked on our first book, *Multiples Illuminated: A Collection of Stories and Advice from Parents of Twins, Triplets and More*, to address a gap in the market. Despite the rising number of multiples born each year, there was a shortage of honest stories and advice to help parents of multiples from pregnancy to the first few years.

Multiples Illuminated: Life with Twins and Triplets, The Toddler to Tween Years offers readers a special look into the lives of parents raising multiples from two to 12 years old.

There is nothing quite like this second book in the *Multiples Illuminated* series. You will read poems, take a hilarious multiple-choice quiz, and experience the joys and challenges of raising multiples through the 21 beautifully written stories. We promise that your experience parenting multiples will be more enriched after reading this anthology.

With the *Multiples Illuminated* books and their accompanying website filled with stories and advice from parents who have been there, we aim to create a welcoming and safe space for families of multiples who are faced with the reality that raising twins, triplets, and more brings unique experiences in comparison to raising singletons. Our community welcomes everyone who wants to know more about multiples.

Make yourself comfortable in your favorite chair, pour a cup of your favorite beverage, and immerse yourself in the pages of this one-of-a-kind book. We will show you just what an illuminating experience it is moving through life with twins and triplets.

Megan and Alison
Editors

INTRODUCTION

ARE YOU READY TO BE A PARENT OF MULTIPLES?

A MULTIPLES-CHOICE TEST

JACKIE PICK

Have you ever said, "I could live at Costco!"?

When you were Octomom for Halloween, could you keep the plastic baby dolls Velcroed to you all night?

Ever feel like you are part of a three-ring circus act?

Take this test to see if you are ready to be a P.O.M., a Parent of Multiples!

Directions: Although this is a 90-minute test, you will be given only seven minutes. You must complete the written part of the exam sitting in a Cheerios-encrusted malodorous minivan while someone kicks the back of your seat. You may bring your test into the bathroom, but don't assume that this will buy you 30 seconds of peace and quiet.

Part 1: Multiple-Choice

Choose the best answer to the following questions.

1. How will you ensure that each of your children gets quality one-on-one time with you?

    a. I'll create a schedule that includes special time each day for each child. All shall abide by this schedule,

11

which will be laminated and posted in convenient places all over the house.

b. I'll do my best to take time with each child every day, but will also take the long view and know that equity will come over a span of days or months.

c. Does eventually dropping them off at college count?

d. I'm supposed to give them one-on-one time?

2. Which child do you go to first when one twin has learned how to undo his diaper and the other has given himself what can only be described as Vicks VapoRub hair?

a. Scoop up the child with the mentholated hair, place safely in the Pack 'n' Play; change the other twin.

b. Plunk both children in the Pack 'n' Play, do another childproofing sweep of the house.

c. Change the diaper. Take photos of the other child's hair; share on social media with tag "Hock (a Loogie) of Seagulls."

d. Grab the duct tape and a washcloth. Improvise.

3. It's Back-to-School night, and the PTA president is chasing you down the hall to be a class mom for one of your multiples. What do you do?

a. Promise her you'll be the class mom for the multiple whose class you didn't do this for last year.

b. Apologize profusely and tell the president that since you can't do it for all your multiples at once, it's best not to do it. Then sign up to chair the bake sale.

c. Duck into the nearest classroom. Odds are one of your children has class in there. Hide there until winter breaks.

d. Laugh. Show the president a picture of your laundry pile. Then cry.

4. A well-meaning individual asks you "Do your triplets have the same personality?" What is the best response?

a. "Yes."

b. "No."

c. "Yes, because that is how people work."

d. "If by 'personality' you mean 'never letting me sit down again,' then, yes."

5. Which expression will most likely make you cry tears of rage?

a. "Double Trouble!/Triple Threat!/Quadruple Craziness!"

b. "Your hands are full!"

c. "Glad it's you and not me."

d. "Sorry, we're closed and there's not another liquor store for 15 miles."

6. A stranger comes up to you in Target during your 23rd week of pregnancy and says, "Oh, good heavens, you're so big!" What is the best response?

a. Return the compliment.

b. "Oh my God, why would you say that? WHY? What is wrong with you?"

 c. Say nothing. Fight back tears. Crumple by the scented candles.

 d. Smile awkwardly and joke about how you do, indeed, feel rather large. Then brood at home into an entire pint of Ben and Jerry's.

8. A different, but not dissimilar stranger approaches you in Target and asks of your multiples, "Are they natural?" What is the best response?

 a. "Yes. Good day, sir."

 b. "No, they're synthetic."

 c. "Before I answer that, would you like to see my episiotomy scar?"

 d. "Yes, they are natural. Are you?"

9. Did you notice there was no question 7 in this section of the test?

 a. Yes! If you look at my answer sheet, you'll see I added my own little question and answers. Then I shared it on Facebook.

 b. No! The important thing is that I am finishing this quiz, no matter what. No. Matter. What. Even if I never sleep again.

 c. Oh, I noticed all right. I didn't want to say anything, but I will make sure to share this attempt at skullduggery with my mommy group.

 d. No. I did not notice. I am tired. I can barely hold this pencil. You're lucky I remembered to wear pants. Wait … yes. I'm wearing pants.

10. What is the best way to get multiples on the same sleep schedule?

    a. Keep them all up, no matter how much they want to fall sleep, until they all are synced.

    b. Put them all down for naps no matter how wide awake they are, until all are synced.

    c. Surrender to the chaos, move next door to a coffee shop, and hope for the best.

    d. What is this 'sleep' you speak of?

Part 2: Math

Show your work.

1. A picture of you feeding your babies (no matter the method) goes viral on social media. How many positive comments will you receive from strangers? How many negative comments will you receive from strangers? How many passive-aggressive comments will you receive from family and friends? What percentage of the comments will be misspelled?

2. A. Using the map provided, plot out a walk in this impossibly family-friendly neighborhood. What is the best route for you to take to lose that baby weight, get some fresh air, get the children out of the house, walk the dog, and pick up some groceries?

    B. Identify these points on the map: Where the children hop out of the stroller; where the dog gets tangled up in shrubbery after chasing a squirrel; where the groceries fall out of the cart; and where the ice cream truck begins to stalk you.

C. Take a dog and one of the strollers filled with children (located at the door), and walk the route you highlighted. This counts as the 'me-time' portion of the test.

Part 3: Short Written Response

Describe a futuristic machine that will sterilize bottles, change diapers, fold laundry, make dinner, and feed multiple crying babies all at once while a spouse asks how they can help.

In 5,000 words or more, explain how three children mysteriously end up in bed with you every morning, despite you tucking them into their own beds each night. Reference Laws of Thermodynamics and Murphy.

Write a letter to the village president describing what specifically it will take to raise your child. Include a list of sitters willing to watch multiples. Then pass that list to the fellow test-taker who has the darkest circles under her eyes.

Part 4: Physical Fitness

1. Transfer all the answers from Section One (multiple-choice) onto a Scantron that we put down somewhere on your kitchen counter a week ago. You have two minutes to retrieve it before the dishes piling up on the counter fall over. Any jelly smudges on the Scantron will be scored as incorrect.

2. In the adjoining room, there is a pot of coffee, a pot of tea, and a bottle of wine. You may have as much of any or all of these as you choose. However, there are five sleeping children between you and that room. Get to the beverages without waking the children. Beware the LEGO and motion-activated talking toys scattered about. You will get partial credit for lying down on the floor and taking a nap alongside the children.

3. Choreograph a dance called 'Taking Multiples to Swim Class' to the tune of 'Mission Impossible.' Go to the playground and perform this dance in front of a panel of judges who will critique your performance and your life choices in a series of passive-aggressive blog posts.

Part 5: Parenting Philosophy

Identify your parenting philosophy in the following areas: feeding, sleeping, potty training, discipline, putting all multiples in separate classes, dual language, STEM education, screen time, and hugging the characters at theme parks. Then debate yourself on all of your deeply held truths, taking both the pro and con positions, one for each twin. If you have, will have, or think you might have three or more children at a time, add additional philosophies as needed. Be sure to pace aimlessly around the classroom clutching your stomach while doing so. Know that if you are wrong, you will damage your children for life.

Part 6: Creativity

1. Describe the following in haiku form:

   • A sippy cup with weeks-old milk found under the couch.

   • Diapers after green beans.

   • Diapers after red beans.

   • Diapers after black beans.

   • The day's first sip of caffeine (yours, not the children's).

   • Having more hungry children than you have nipples.

2. The proctor will play a recording of a cacophonous assault on your brain. Identify each of the following: Three children and what they are asking for/crying

about; the UPS man's delivery time; the phone call and who it is; which electronic toy is broken and stuck on making barnyard noises and which barnyard noises are being made; what food is exploding in the microwave; which neighbor is blowing leaves; and whether this is just a test of the emergency broadcast system or an actual emergency.

3. Using scented markers, draw a political cartoon based on the pithy maxim, "Someday you'll miss this." Be sure to include and label the following elements:

• Bags under your eyes.

• Vomit or other bodily fluids on your shirt.

• How many days it has been since you've showered.

• Pop culture character worn or carried by your child, and specifically when you capitulated and bought it for them.

• Halo over the person making that remark.

• Your preferred method of torturing that person.

Scoring: Hand in your test to the sour-looking person at the back of the room. She will gleefully tell you that you are wrong, without even glancing at your work. Thank her for her opinion, and then ponder the fact that you will never have all the answers.

Give yourself exactly zero points …

…which is all to say that you are in no way ready to have multiples.

Extra Credit: Have multiples anyway.

Jackie Pick is a former teacher and current word monkey living in the Chicago area with her husband, three children, and a very fuzzy dog. She is a contributing author to Multiples Illuminated: A Collection of Stories and Advice from Parents of Twins, Triplets and More, So Glad They Told Me: Women Get Real about Motherhood, Here in the Middle, *as well as the literary magazine* Selfish. *Her writing has been featured on various sites including Mamalode, The HerStories Project, and Scary Mommy. Jackie is also the co-creator and co-writer of the upcoming short film* Bacon Wrapped Dates, *and occasionally performs sketch and musical comedy in Chicago.*

ARE YOU READY TO BE A PARENT OF MULTIPLES?

THE TODDLER YEARS

TODDLER TIPS AND ADVICE

ALISON LEE

Toddlerhood is challenging for both children and parents, and the difficulties of this developmental stage appear amplified with twins or triplets. Typically at this stage, parents deal with potty training, tantrums, increasing independence, and boundary-pushing. The ages of two to three are also when children are learning to express themselves and their strong emotions.

Having had two singletons before twins, I thought I was fully equipped to handle the toddler stage.

I was wrong.

I did not anticipate the constant fighting for toys and attention. I had no idea how to manage two simultaneous meltdowns. I became nervous about taking them out on my own because I was worried they would run off in different directions, or ask to be carried at the same time. One crying child in a restaurant is tough enough – two, it's a disaster.

If you thought only teenagers get moody, you must have forgotten what the toddler stage is like. They go from zero to 100 on the mood spectrum. They swing from happy to angry, back to happy, in a matter of seconds. My two and a half-year-old daughter once threw an epic 45-minute tantrum for reasons unknown to me (that's two challenges wrapped in one – a tantrum and trying to figure out why and how to resolve it). I'm not one for bribes, but in desperation, I offered her ice cream. Her tears dried up immediately, and her face lit up. Smiling, she nodded demurely, and all was well again. Toddlers are unpredictable, so don't expect the same tactic to work again.

However, it's not all doom and gloom. This stage is fun for the most part, and watching your multiples learning together is amazing. My boy/girl twins are inseparable. When one is not around, the other goes looking for him or her. They are always thinking of each other – when one twin gets a treat, they always make sure to get one for the other. Watching them communicate is both hilarious and heartwarming.

Since they turned two, and are now edging to three, I've gained some experience in managing some, if not all of the challenges in raising twin toddlers. My top tips on surviving and thriving this stage are:

- To prevent your multiples from fighting over things like water bottles, utensils, and the like, designate them their own plates, spoons, cups, and water bottles by color. I've used this tactic since my twins were babies, and it works!

- When you have more than one child, spending one-on-one time with each one is a challenge. Add in the fact that your children are twins or triplets, and you'll find this nearly impossible. I overcome this by teaching them to take turns. We all play together, but they take turns with me in whatever game we're playing. This way, they get a dash of one-on-one time, and everyone's having fun.

- Encourage them to do separate activities occasionally, and with other kids, be it other siblings, cousins, or friends. Twins and triplets are usually rather insular, having a built-in playmate, and don't know how to get along with someone other than each other. Take this as an opportunity to encourage independence from each other, albeit in small doses.

• When it comes to dealing with potty training or teaching them to express themselves, remember to treat your multiples as individuals. They will not always be learning at the same pace. Do not compare your twins or triplets.

• For parents of multiples, crying toddlers is a reality we quickly come to accept. Sometimes, we have to just let them cry. We can only deal with and handle one child at a time for most things, the other will have to wait. Don't stress out, it's normal. Remember that there is no such thing as equal when it comes to multiples. You can only be fair. That means, you look after the needs of each child as and when they need it. Honor their individual needs.

• Take a break from your children. I would suggest you do this regularly. If you have support and help, take advantage of that, and do something for yourself. Go to the gym for 30 minutes, or take a one-hour lunch break. Or once a month, have a girls' night out with your friends. You need to look after you, too.

There is no magic formula to get through the toddler stage. The year between the time they turn two and when they celebrate their third birthday might feel like an eternity. However, it's a privilege to be a parent of multiples. Watching the unique relationship between them is the magic you need to get through this time. You don't have to love every minute, but you can enjoy the overall experience. You *can* survive this stage!

THE CHECKUP

SHANNA SILVA

You double-check your bag: snacks, juice boxes, Toy Story Action Figures. You are ready. Your twin boys are dressed in matching outfits in different colors. Their teeth are brushed. Their jackets are zipped. You give yourself a cursory look in the mirror on the way out the door. You notice the coffee stain on the hem of your shirt, and you tuck the offending corner into your pants.

You buckle the boys into their car seats and hope they don't fall asleep on the ride to the doctor's office. They are often unpleasant when awoken. In fact, they can be inconsolable. And if one cries, the other joins in out of solidarity. You are outnumbered.

You score a parking space near the office! You will not need to pray that someone will hold the door open as you wedge your double stroller through the narrow doorframe. You check into the front desk and are sent to the 'healthy kids' waiting room. You notice the kid with the snotty nose and cough is playing with the healthy-side toys while her mother chats on her cell phone. You judge her a little.

You try to entice the boys with the toys you've brought from home, but they are only interested in the germy waiting room toys. You give up and watch *Finding Nemo* on the screen. There is no volume.

You endure the usual questions from strangers who are so verbally thankful they only have one child at a time. Yes, they are twins. No, they're not identical (they look nothing alike!). You pause at the query about twins running in your family. Do you really feel like sharing your infertility/IVF story with a total stranger? You cannot believe how often you are asked this intrusive question. You decide to say that twins run in your family (at least they do now).

You run interference between your boys, who both want to ride on the big wheel. You tell them that it's broken – they must play with something else. Your appointment was scheduled to begin 15 minutes ago. You put on a pitiful face as you check in again with the receptionist. You know she can move things along if she really wants to. And you know that there is a solid chance of a meltdown in the next 10 minutes. It's anyone's guess whether it will be from you or the kids.

You are finally called into an exam room, and you are relieved to be in the train-decorated room, not the princess-decorated room. Like last time. You try to entertain the boys and pass the time by playing *I Spy*. They are bored within two minutes. They both want your lap. But you are sitting in a child-sized chair with your knees up around your ears. You lift them up onto the exam table and sit between them. You find some crayons and draw together on the medical table white paper.

The boys are making fist-sized holes in the paper and you have to pee. You calculate you will have to hold it in for at least another hour. The doctor enters, full of cheer for their well check. You answer questions about their development while the boys make fart noises. You blush when one of your four-year-old twins uses the word 'shit.' Appropriately.

You hold one wiggly boy while the other is examined. You try to make a mental note of his weight and height, but the numbers escape your frazzled brain within seconds. You trade boys with the doctor and struggle to remember your questions. You are pleased to remember one of the four. The other three will hit you in the parking lot.

Your thoughts drift as you plan what you will do later while (if) they nap. Laundry, emails, dishes, a cup of coffee, dinner preparation. But you know you will watch T.V. and drift to sleep, sitting up with your head bobbing.

You bring yourself back to the present. The exams are over. Your boys are healthy. One is in the 90th percentile for weight, one is in the 55th. You make a mental note to toss the Goldfish and sugary fruit snacks.

The doctor mouths the word "vaccine." He turns his back to prepare, and you notice the panic in your kids' eyes. They miss nothing, and they hate needles. Do not underestimate them.

Mr. 55th percentile makes a run for the door, and makes it down the hallway. Mr. 90th is running around the room, shrieking. You know the people in the waiting room hear him. So do the people in the adjacent grocery store. Everyone is judging you.

You retrieve your 55th percentile track star, close and lock the door. Sweat is pooling in your bra. Your heart is pulsating. You think you will open a nice Chardonnay later because you will need it after this.

You quietly curse your husband for being at work while you are double-teamed at the pediatrician. He is probably having a leisurely business lunch, laughing, and wearing clean clothes.

You remember when you used to work: running a department, fielding client requests, traveling, writing newsletters, meeting deadlines, making presentations, soliciting investments. This is much harder.

You sheepishly grin at the doctor, hoping that this inoculation-revolt is a common occurrence. He tells you to hold one boy still while he comes in closer with the shot. You notice your four-year-old is incredibly strong, and you end up wrestling and pinning him to the floor. As the doctor closes in, you brace yourself because with all the squirming, you might end up getting the needle yourself. And that would really suck. Because you would still have to get the shot into his arm.

You cringe at the scream that escapes from your cherub's lips. You are fully sweating now, and worry your pits smell. You may have forgotten deodorant today.

You ready the second boy as the first chooses his Band-Aid. He selects Spider-Man. You hope there is another for his brother.

You avoid being pricked with the needle and are still thinking about your reward Chardonnay. The screams die down. The tears stop.

There are no more Spider-Man Band-Aids. Your son settles for Sponge Bob, but lets you know he is not happy.

The boys choose lollipops, and you grab one for yourself. Root Beer – the flavor no one else likes. You wish it were a cup of coffee.

You pay your co-pay and corral the boys. You pick them up and balance one on each hip. You are super strong, and you have no idea that in 10 years your hips will ache and you will go to physical therapy, and no one will be able to figure out why.

You buckle them into their car seats and sit in the driver's seat, trying to calm yourself. You call your husband to tell him the story but find your words really don't express the absurdity and stress of the situation. You resolve to dump the kids in his arms as soon as he gets home, so you can go for a walk.

You get home and bring the boys into the house. Your feet crunch the Cheerios you didn't get a chance to pick up. You put in a video for the boys – the one they have seen hundreds of times. You know it by heart and find yourself singing the lyrics. You load the dishwasher and realize you missed lunch, and settle for a cheese stick and animal crackers. Your diet will start tomorrow.

You climb on the couch, thoroughly spent from the day's antics. Your boys curl up next to you. Their hair smells like baby shampoo and you drink it in. You put your arms around them and hold them close. They look at you with pure love. This is your real reward, not the wine (although you will have that, too). They are yours, the best part of you. You are the center of their world.

You worry that when they grow up, they will get married and forget you.

Your husband comes home full of energy and pep. You haven't felt that way in a long time and you wonder if you ever will again.

He jokes about your experience at the doctor's office and you fight the urge to kick him.

It's too soon to laugh about it.

Maybe tomorrow.

Shanna Silva is an author, freelance writer and two-time Tony-nominated Broadway producer. In addition to writing for the parenting blog, Kveller, her work can be found in Chicken Soup for the Soul and Multiples Illuminated. *Shanna is also the author of* Passover Scavenger Hunt *(2017) and has two more children's books in the publication process. Shanna lives in a lively, noisy house with her husband and three amazing children in Long Island, New York.*

THE TODDLER YEARS

POOP IS COMING!

EMILY LINDBLAD

We were at a wildlife sanctuary. The sun was shining, the birds were singing and my energetic three-year-old triplets, who had started to protest naps, were hopefully tiring themselves out. This was a place we visited frequently, with miles of trails, animals we read about in books, an enormous working farm, and no shortage of space for three curious explorers to roam. The sanctuary was filled with other rambunctious children and their slightly harried parents, who also knew the crushing disappointment of the pig barn being closed.

My trio could be counted on to stick together and listen about as well as three semi-tame raccoons, making this a place where I felt reasonably confident taking them by myself. Gone were the days when I had to beg assistance from family or friends to successfully complete a trip to the grocery store without meltdowns – theirs or mine. The three amigos were potty trained to the point that I felt comfortable taking them out in public wearing underwear. They were very proud of their 'big kid' status and happily used the bathroom before we set off to explore some of the more rugged parts of the sanctuary. We hiked and chatted about bugs and trees and fire trucks. Overall, it was a very pleasant morning together.

Then, disaster struck.

"Poop is coming!"

"You're right, I bet that chipmunk would love to be your friend. Hold on a sec, what did your sister say?"

"Poop is coming RIGHT NOW!"

"Now, *now?*"

"RIGHT NOW!"

"Okay," I said, "Do you think we have time to make it back to the bathroom or do you need to find somewhere to go around here?" Coincidentally, 'nature pees' are my son's favorite pastime.

"NO! I can't poop in the woods!" Unfortunately, my daughter does not share her brother's view of the great outdoors as a scenic public toilet.

We quickly packed up the picnic lunch that we had just unpacked, spilling half of the Craisins, making that chipmunk's day. I made sure everyone had a sandwich to eat en route to the toilet, proceeded back over the river and through the woods to grandmother's house – I mean the one public restroom that was two miles away.

For a while, everyone tagged along dutifully, marshaled by their sister's frequent, and loud, reminders that "poop is coming!" We reached the intersection of the path where, steps away, just on the other side of the trees, beckoning like a new season of *Orange Is the New Black* on Netflix, was the bathroom. One child started to run down the path as fast as her little legs could carry her, the second stopped to look at a rock, and the third stopped dead in his tracks and decided he wasn't going to go any further.

"No, I don't want to go that way," complete with foot stomp for emphasis.

"Hey, look, shiny!" while poking in the dirt at the side of the trail.

"POOP! POOP IS COMING!" she said, hand over bottom, ponytail swinging in time to a very awkward run.

Cajoling/bribery/threats commenced as I tried to herd two unwilling children and one anxious pooper toward the restrooms. As we slowly made progress, one of the sanctuary staff members was walking up the trail.

"Oh wow, are those triplets?"

Are we seriously having this conversation now?! I don't mind stopping for a quick chat about my kids, but *seriously, lady, does this look like the time?*

"Yes, they are. It's always an adventure," I responded as I resorted to carrying one ticking time bomb, dragging the protester by the hand, and hoping the future geologist would follow along once she realized she could just pick the damn rock up and bring it with her.

"Oh cool! I have twins," said the well-meaning yet clearly oblivious employee as she continued to stand in the middle of the path that leads to poo-vana. "I can't imagine what having three would be like."

"Want one?" I joked as I tried to maneuver the four of us around her.

"That's so funny, have a great day!" She waved and trotted happily off, continuing with her blissful, I-don't-have-to-wipe-another-human's-butt-right-now day.

Everyone in the state now knew that a bowel movement was imminent, that some siblings believed bathroom trips weren't meant to be a group experience, and that the sparkly stone had been dropped and lost among the 203,856 other rocks on the ground.

We finally barged inside the (thankfully vacant) restroom, plopped the pooper down on the toilet, and waited.

And waited ... "Don't touch that!"

And waited. *I'd kill for a drink right now.*

Until at last, the tiniest, daintiest toot broke the silence.

"Hey, Mama, I guess it was just gas."

Emily Lindblad is a postpartum doula, newborn care specialist, and mother of triplets. She lives with her family outside of Boston, Massachusetts and believes that her children's current goal in life is to try out every public toilet in the state.

THE TODDLER YEARS

SO MUCH MORE

BRITON UNDERWOOD

As my twins grew, I worried about how their popularity might affect them. From the time they were born, they have constantly captivated a public audience. They've always been the center of attention. In the NICU, nurses fought to cover their room. At the grocery store, people abruptly stopped to take in the sight of twins. People flocked to their presence, showering them with attention.

They knew it, too. When we were out, they always acted overdramatic. They laughed a little harder, fought a little more, and got into each other's faces more than usual. Being the center of attention was something they came to enjoy. It is a part of who they are and they basked in their main attraction uniqueness. Feeding off other people's excitement, their grins grew bigger each time they heard someone squeal the magic word excitedly.

"TWINS!"

But while they were enjoying their performance, someone's little feet dragged behind them. The youngest son. The singleton. He was as aware of the act as they were. The first time I watched someone ignore my youngest child to gawk at the twins, I visibly cringed. It hurt to think his life will always be the younger brother to the twin show.

"Twins!" The magic word comes out, followed by an awkward, "Oh! And another ..."

I wasn't the only one to notice the less-than-spectacular treatment of baby boy. It sparked something in my little attention seekers.

They no longer traipsed hand in hand down the aisles. Instead, they opted to get on either side of their brother. As they pulled him into their act, I no longer began to worry about how their popularity might affect him. They began to giggle, as the magic word was replaced with a new, better word.

"Triplets?!?!"

It sparked laughter in the whole family. The silly assumption that the boy in the middle who is a full foot shorter was born at the same time. Even at their young age, my boys understand the absurdity. Yet, people continue to be fooled. And my youngest? He no longer trudges along behind the act. He has become a part of the show.

There are things we strive to teach our children, whether we have multiples or singletons. One of those things, maybe the biggest of them, is the importance of inclusion. Some of my proudest moments as a parent are watching my twins share the spotlight with their little brother. Their understanding of how important it is to make sure everyone feels special is something I hope will continue to grow healthily, along with their little bodies.

Even now, as they go to school, I get reports of how good my twins are. How they enjoy helping people on the playground and holding hands with their friends. They are in separate classes, yet at recess can be found adding people into their little special theater.

My twins are special. They are miracle babies who came into this world early, kicking and screaming. They have their twin-speak conversations and matching mannerisms. Their best similarity, though, doesn't come from their appearance. It's their hearts. It's their ability to see what is important in the world, maybe a bit better than most adults.

I spent a lot of time worrying about how my twins' popularity might affect them. What they would become from the constant attention. I worried about how their ability to turn heads would affect their little brother. What would happen as person after person pushed him to the side for a better look at the twin show. Would my youngest learn to just hang back? To trudge along, out of the way?

People will always notice my oldest boys for being twins. It is who they are and it is a special, beautiful, bond they have. I wouldn't want to change that, nor could anyone else. But, as I watch them interlock arms with their brother, I beam with pride, knowing they would rather share their special spotlight than bask in it by themselves.

I watch my boys run up to their brother, get on each side of him and take up the whole aisle. As they strut and gain attention, seeking out the magic world from onlookers. It always fills me with joy.

They aren't just the twin show. They are so much more.

Briton Underwood, better known as Punk Rock Papa, is a parent above all else. When he gets sick of being at their beck and call, he likes to escape to his page or site. He writes about any and everything he wants, but mainly about his twin boys or his newest addition – another boy. He also would like the world to know he has a beautiful wife, because the couch isn't that comfy.

A TALE OF TWO SISSIES

MAUREEN BONATCH

"You've dressed them alike. Who are you?" Sueann knelt to face the blonde, brown-eyed girl clinging to my leg.

Responding on cue, Laken lifted her bangs to reveal a brown beauty mark.

"That's Laken." I nudged Yasmine, my other blonde, brown-eyed cherub, forward. "This is Yasmine. I can't take credit for the outfits. My girls have dressed themselves since they were eighteen months old."

"Independent gals, then?"

"That's an understatement." They'd already discovered every forbidden crevice in our house.

"You girls are going to have so much fun in daycare!" Sueann clapped her hands together with the unnatural glee only educators of small children possess.

"Call me if you have any trouble." I regarded my two-year old twins with apprehension. They appeared innocent and subdued, but once the initial shyness faded, their curiosity was insatiable.

"Maureen, don't worry about us at all," Sueann shook her finger at me and clasped Yasmine's hand, then Laken's. "Tell your mama you'll be fine, girls."

Laken and Yasmine spotted the toy-filled room and their eyes widened. They nodded in agreement and rushed in to explore the treasures. I was already forgotten.

I drove home with a knot in my stomach. *My babies were away from home for the first time.* It was for the best. Even the pediatrician recommended enrolling the twins in daycare. They'd been either competing with each other or trying to kill each other, since birth.

The ringing of the phone interrupted my uncommonly quiet morning. "Hello?"

"Maureen? It's Sueann, from daycare."

Only two hours had passed since I dropped the girls off. I envisioned this as the first of many calls over the coming years from teachers and school administrators. "What happened?" I steeled myself for the worst.

"I'm having a little problem," Sueann chuckled.

I cringed and waited to hear what terror my two had inflicted upon the unsuspecting class. Past incidents of the twins include teething on each other, teaching one another to climb out of the crib and how to scale the cabinets onto the counters, rifling through the medicine cabinet, and their attempts at doing laundry. Apparently two heads *are* better than one.

"I'm really embarrassed to even say this, but," Sueann hesitated. "I don't know which one is which."

I released my breath. "The beauty mark—"

"I know, I know," Sueann continued, "I forgot which girl has the beauty mark. So I asked one of them their name. She said, *Sissy.* Then I asked her what her sister's name was and she said, *Sissy.* They both think their name is Sissy."

The heat of a blush climbed my neck. When we brought the identical babies home from the hospital, I feared having to return to establish the correct identity of baby A and baby B.

To avoid confusing them, I painted Yasmine's toenail red. After weeks of swaddling all of Yasmine but her big toe, we decided the strawberry birthmark on her forehead was here to stay. This worked well for confirming who was who for the first six months, until their hair grew. Luckily, Laken sprouted a beauty mark on her forehead, providing us with our latest method of positive identification.

Even so, much of our family had taken to referring to the other sibling as *Sissy*. They found it easier than trying to ensure they knew which twin they were talking to. After all of our efforts to ensure our identical twins had an individual identity, they didn't even know their own name. My shoulders fell.

"Um," I muttered, "Laken has the beauty mark. I'll be sure they dress differently tomorrow. Yasmine in yellow and Laken in lavender."

By the end of the week, each time anyone got within a yard of Laken, she anticipated their next move and held up her bangs to reveal her beauty mark. Apparently, no one in the daycare was getting any better at telling them apart.

One night, I lay awake, mustering up the energy to get out of bed. Two years old and the girls still didn't sleep through the night.

"One of the girls is crying," Jamie poked my side.

"It's Yasmine." I hauled my legs over the edge of the bed.

"How can you tell?" Jamie rolled over to resume his slumber.

"Yasmine is always the one up with nightmares. I don't have to see them to know that." I gaped. I knew there were differences between the girls that were more than skin deep. Their personalities were like night and day. I just had to make everyone aware of their subtle nuances. Perhaps then Laken wouldn't be constantly patted on the head as people discretely searched for the beauty mark.

I arrived at daycare the next day with a plan. "Yasmine is a little more outgoing than Laken," I said to Sueann.

Yasmine proudly displayed her T-shirt, which announced her birth order.

"You're the big sister I see," Sueann smiled.

"Laken is 14 minutes younger than Yasmine." I handed Laken back her stuffed toy. "As you can see, Laken is left-handed, while Yasmine is right-handed."

Sueann laughed. "Should I be taking notes?"

I ran my hand through my hair in frustration. "I want the girls to feel like individuals. I want them to know their own name, and not be identified by a color or a facial feature."

"They do," Sueann tilted her head. "*You* can tell them apart, that's obvious just seeing you with them. Others will learn with time."

"I've been trying to call them by name more often . . ."

"Parents are always their own worst critic." She patted my arm in reassurance. "We enrolled *two* girls for daycare. Two girls who know who they are, but may like their nickname of *Sissy*. It probably makes them feel special," Sueann shrugged, "Besides, this will probably be one of the smallest problems you'll have in their lifetime."

I looked at my twins. Laken was holding Yasmine's hand but discreetly pinching her finger. Yasmine shoved her back. "I'm sure you're right."

We both laughed as we envisioned the future years, although I suspect Sueann may have been laughing at me rather than with me.

Maureen Bonatch grew up in small-town Pennsylvania and her love of the four seasons—hockey, biking, sweat pants and hibernation—keeps her there. While immersed in writing or reading paranormal romance and fantasy, she survives on caffeine, wine, music, and laughter. A feisty Shih Tzu, her teen twins and alpha hubby keep her in line.

WHEN ONE TWIN HAS CANCER

JESSICA MARTINEAU

Our lives changed on a single day in January 2016.

The entire morning was a blur. We'd left our three girls, Presley four, and Ava and Mila, identical 16-month old twins, at home with their grandmother. My husband, Mark, and I knew we should bring our full attention to the team of doctors we were scheduled to meet with that day.

I knew deep down that the request to review Mila's scans at the Jimmy Fund Clinic of the Dana Farber Cancer Institute in Boston was not a sign of good news. I held out hope but my heart felt heavy.

"You know, this is where cancer patients go for treatment …"

Silence.

"Seems funny to ask us to come here if this wasn't cancer."

"Let's just go and see what they have to say, okay?"

My husband remaining level-headed. Not worrying until there was something to worry about. His words said one thing but his expression another.

At that point, we knew that making assumptions for the next hour or so was a pointless and disheartening task. We remained quiet for the remainder of the ride.

As we walked into the clinic, I briefly scanned the room and immediately diverted my eyes to the floor. Was this about to become our home away from home? I did not want

Mark or any of the patients or parents to see the emotion building in my eyes.

There were young children, obviously patients of the clinic, playing with toys or crafting. Friendly-faced parents, grandparents, and caretakers that looked at us all too knowingly. Like they knew something we had yet to become aware of.

I am not one of you, I thought to myself.

We were whisked into a private room filled with a team of people. Brief introductions later, we had met Mila's oncologist team. Doctors, surgeons, social workers, and nurses.

The pediatric oncologist, a young-looking man, warm by default, Dr. X, took the lead.

"Jessica, Mark ... we received the results of the biopsy. Mila has Embryonal Rhabdomyosarcoma."

That was the scary medical term for what was a large tumor I'd discovered on Mila's right hip during a routine trip to tubby time.

He proceeded to inform us that this was a rare and aggressive form of cancer.

Mark put his hand to his face and tears fell. I had never seen him like this before, and it scared me. I must have missed something. I was not following. There were so many solemn eyes looking at us. Awaiting a response. I felt like a deer caught in headlights.

Dr. X continued, "We will begin with surgery to remove the tumor and the muscle surrounding it. From there, we will decide her specific treatment plan. It is definitive that she will receive weekly chemotherapy for 12 months. The pending factor will be the addition of radiation. This will be an unknown until we see what we are dealing with."

The reference to chemotherapy hit me like a boulder. As I started to lose it, Mark began to compose himself. It was as if we passed off the strength baton.

This was the moment we were welcomed into the family we never wanted to be a part of.

Immediately after Mila's diagnosis, Ava popped into my mind. Was this her impending doom? Would she get cancer now? Or after Mila finished her treatment? Years down the road, would we hit the repeat button? We needed to know if this disease was genetic, because our twins are identical.

Our worries were laid to rest later when a genetic test proved that this cancer did not develop from a genetic strand. Ava as well as Presley, had as slim a chance of developing cancer as any other healthy child. The other silver lining of this diagnosis was a recent study that confirmed that a six-month treatment would be just as effective as a year-long one. Just like that, Mila was halfway through.

After a successful surgery, Mila began her journey of weekly chemotherapy. It was the first time she and her twin had been separated for several days. Ava spent the day with her grandmother and Mila received sole attention from me. They both loved the one-on-one time. However, the moment we walked in the door on Wednesday evenings, they ran to each other and commemorated the reunion with joyful squeals.

Every third Wednesday, Mila came home with a hydration backpack and was on a strong, continued, dosage of anti-nausea drugs that caused her to be a bit loopy. The hydration backpack was connected to her through a port in her chest. It had about two feet of slack. On these evenings, Mila, Ava and I would curl up into a chair together and watch *Curious George* for a few short hours until bedtime. Ava, having the flexibility to be up and about if needed, would grab her water bottle or a banana for herself and Mila just in case she wanted it. She was unapologetically thoughtful and supportive, as if she knew how her sister was feeling.

The mornings Mila woke up in her crib after sleeping with the hydration backpack were not the easiest. The medicine made her nauseated, and occasionally she would vomit. As I tended to Mila to get her clean and comfortable, Ava waited patiently in her crib. When Mila was cleaned up, I would place her in Ava's crib to continue cleaning the rest of the room. The girls sat contentedly together. Despite not understanding the seriousness of cancer, Ava became her sister's safe space and kept her smiling. When the twins were together, you would never have known Mila had cancer and was undergoing a treatment that could bring a 200-pound man to his knees.

Together, with Presley and Ava's support, love and laughter kicked this disease to the curb.

The entire time, Mark and I tried to stay ahead of the worries that came with battling childhood cancer. We took it one day at a time. We followed her regimen intently and tried to keep our routine as normal as possible. We did not cater to Mila more than we did Presley and Ava. On Wednesdays, we dealt with our cancer to-do list. We followed her medication plan and responded to her as needed when she was feeling under the weather.

Our family had a community of support. If and when Mila ran a temperature that forced an impromptu trip to the hospital for immediate attention, the girls were understanding and excited for the visit of a grandparent or neighbor. The individual attention brought Presley and Ava joy in a time of worry.

One condition with Mila's treatment plan was that she was to be more secluded from people than usual because her immune system could not handle any additional battles with germs. Mark and I hired Mila a nanny, Joan, who was going to spend time with her every morning while Presley, Ava, and I continued with our regular routine. Presley attended preschool three days a week while Ava and I visited the gym and playroom. I worked out and was able to be semi-sociable for a brief period of time. Exercise cleared my head and kept me going mentally while Ava spent time in a social setting playing with friends and releasing some energy. Meanwhile, Mila basked in the friendship that bloomed between her and Joan. They went on walks and Mila was treated like a princess.

Mark maintained a regular work schedule and we continued to pass the baton of strength back and forth. From the time the cancer diagnosis came, we would not allow ourselves to feel the full weight of realization that one of our babies had cancer. We did not give in to the fear that we could lose her. It simply was not an option: I repeat, not an option. We fortified ourselves for the fight ahead. We knew we had to be strong for our girls. Remaining positive and happy was the strongest power we had against this disease.

We told friends and family that Mila was a fighter. We updated them regularly with straightforward situational information and continued to inform them that Mila was getting through this with unbelievable strength, positivity, and grace. We let them know that their combined support made our family stronger. Never had I realized the size of the circle of compassion, strength, and unlimited support that surrounded our family. It was an astonishing force that kept us going.

Six months after that dreadful day in January, Mila's PET scan was clear. She is cancer-free, remission being the technical term. The treatment worked.

Ava and Mila continue to be a force to be reckoned with. At no point in this journey did Mila walk alone. The twins continue to be the best of friends, typical bickering-and-hair-pulling-sisters (this time Mila's hair doesn't come out in Ava's hand), a devilish mattress-flipping combo, and beyond thoughtful for one another. And that shall remain through sickness and health.

Jessica Martineau is a freelance writer, avid blogger, workout-nut, foodie, and lover of all things wine. Jessica's writing is inspired by her family that continues to grow. She is the mother of four girls, Presley, identical twins Ava and cancer survivor Mila, and latest addition, Lenin. Her work portrays the full spectrum of the realities of motherhood and she shares stories of the joys, fears, aggravations, and heartache of parenting on her blog, Breaking the Momma Mold.

GO TIME

CARYN BERARDI

The first time I cried at daycare pickup, we were experiencing a rare August thunderstorm in Dallas. One of my twin boys (the runner) had already broken loose from my grip three times before we could even exit the facility. My other son insisted on being held.

I had worn a dress to work that day because even if it's raining, the temperature in late summer in Texas feels like 10 Bikram yoga classes. With two little backpacks on my shoulders — proudly boasting my children's names in Sharpie marker instead of the more elegant embroidery of some of their classmates — I was chasing and scooping and trying not to flash my everything to the innocent parents and kids talking about their day as they calmly walked from the door to their cars. At least this is how the scene played out through my self-conscious and embarrassed eyes.

By the time one of the school administration staff helped me by physically blocking one child from running into the busy parking lot while I got the other one in the car seat, plump tears were rolling down my face.

Later that night, after my boys were asleep and my mind was able to recalibrate to its resting state, the realization hit me: we were not going to be the exception. The boys were two and-a-half-years-old, and while our first few months of their third year were not terrible, halfway through, they had finally gotten the memo; it was go time.

Now, every daycare pickup was fraught with battles to get to the car. They would only wear one set of pajamas and one pair of sweatpants (did I mention it was summer in Texas?). And even though the sweatpants were *identical*, one twin always had to have their brother's pair. A pout had become the default expression, forming on their faces as soon as they realized the sun was up.

None of these behaviors are uncommon for toddlers. In fact, they are developmentally appropriate, especially for twins who have a built-in partner in crime, as well as a foe to play off of. Of course, there were many tender moments intertwined with the chaos (always at just the right time before you walk outside to get the mail and forget to come back).

The issue is that, while I would never say it aloud, I was honestly convinced we would get through the twos with minimal toddler-isms. Both of my sons are low-key in nature, a trait they inherited from their father. Sure, they bickered over toys and changed their opinion on what they would eat between every meal, but they listened. They slept. They didn't fuss or cry very often outside of expected situations. They wore whatever I put on them. I'm not attributing any of these behaviors to extraordinary parenting techniques, just pure personality and temperament.

In short, they tricked me.

Or perhaps, I tricked myself. Tricked myself into thinking that toddler horror stories were not much different from the horror stories my friends and I told each other during middle school sleepovers in a dark room with a flashlight — enough to scare you and give you nightmares, but never going to happen.

Looking back, I believe these delusions were actually a self-preservation mechanism. A healthy dose of denial that allows you to get through each stage of raising multiples with the assurance that the next stage will be easier.

The other morning, I watched on the monitor as my boys stood up in their cribs, having one of their private conversations that only they and their beloved stuffed animals, Piggy and Moo Moo, were privy to. The endearing scene dissolved into tears when in a dramatic expression of excitement, Piggy was thrown out of the crib away from my son's reach. Desperate cries of "Mooooooooommy" replaced the giggles from a second earlier. I got out of bed. It was go time.

This scene would never have happened before they turned two, when they barely seemed to notice each other. Before they turned two, my son – the runner, but also a sensitive soul who feels everything around him – would never ask his brother if he was okay when he fell down. And I wouldn't have the daily honor of watching them discover who they are – as brothers and as individuals – in a way that is profoundly different from the infant years.

As we near the end of the twos, daycare pickup continues to mimic a corrupt political deal, full of negotiations, threats to walk away, and bribes. We were definitely not the exception when it came to twin toddler antics, but accepting that has better prepared us for what's to come. Like the first time you spill coffee in a new car, you are initially crushed, but it actually relieves a lot of stress because you are no longer worried about the first stain. I don't hold out hope that we will defy any challenging stage in years to come; my strategy now is simply to embrace it and move forward.

That said, I'm really not worried about this whole 'threenager' thing. No way is that happening to us.

Caryn Berardi works in higher education and is passionate about helping students grow both personally and professionally. She tries to do the same at home, but her toddler twin boys don't listen very well. Caryn lives in Texas with her family and her writing has been seen on The Huffington Post, Kveller, Grown and Flown, Scary Mommy, Beyond Your Blog and Modern Loss.

BETTER TOGETHER

ALISON LEE

Toddlers are sweet, yes?
Twins multiply the good times
Double the cuddles.

Double cuddles, but
Everything else quadruples
Baths, feeds, dressing them.

Here we go again
The breaking up of conflict
Stress level's at ten.

Screams reverberate
Two voices ring in anger
Twins fighting again.

Here she comes running
In my lap she goes, always
He follows, upset.

Arms outstretched – me, me!
I reach out to him, hey you
Her leg, his head, kick!

He flops on the floor
Life, unfair when there are two
I feel you, too, bud.

Two arms, one big heart
Still, it doesn't seem enough
For my twin toddlers.

Entwined forever
From in utero to birth
Better together.

But each wants Mama
For themselves and to themselves
Better apart, yes?

Let's do one-on-one
Sister goes to grandparents
Brother stays with me.

"She was unhappy."
Surprise report from grandma
"She missed her brother."

Not better apart
How do we do *together*?
One Mom, two small ones.

Not a thing is fair
Nothing is equal, nothing
What a conundrum.

Whatever he gets
He makes sure she has one too
Comes naturally.

Whatever she gets
She asks for one for him too
How else could it be?

Nicknames for each twin
A result of toddler talk
Something that's their own.

"Where are you?" he says
"Here, me!" They play hide-and-seek
Hugs when each is found.

When it comes to food
Everything must be equal
No more and no less.

But this is real life
I can't measure perfectly
So it's more or less.

More or less it is
With my time and attention
Such is life, I say.

"Bath time!" I call out
Protests aplenty of course
Sweat and dirt be damned.

Cajole them I do
Straight into the rain shower
Squeals of delight, whee!

They splash, splosh, and splish
I watch as their hands and feet
Move in unison.

Come on out, darlings
Protests aplenty of course
We are having fun!

Out they come at last
Into their pajamas, phew
I'm spent, they are not.

He wants me to read
Picks a book, sits on my lap
Head under my chin.

The peace is broken
When she waves her book at me
And asks for space, too.

I scoot him over
She squishes in next to him
Two heads, one full lap.

Even reading is
Not a simple thing for us
Each wants their book read.

"We'll take turns!" I say
That is futile as usual
Reading is a farce.

"Come on, guys," I plead
Let's read together, both books
Hah! As if, as if.

They tear at the books
Mine first, mine first, tempers flare
I sit, defeated.

Finally, I say
I'll read one page of his book
Then one from yours, girl.

They relent at last
Story time is twice as long
But at least, peaceful.

They sleep together
Huddled heads, dreaming, peaceful
Hands and feet a tangle.

We love them the same
Not one more, not another less
Immeasurable love.

Alison Lee is the co-editor of Multiples Illuminated: A Collection of Stories and Advice from Parents of Twins, Triplets and More, *a writer, and publisher. Alison's writing has been featured in Mamalode, On Parenting at The Washington Post, The Huffington Post, Everyday Family, Scary Mommy, and Club Mid. She is a contributor to two anthologies,* My Other Ex: Women's True Stories of Leaving and Losing Friends *and* So Glad They Told Me: Women Get Real About Motherhood. *Alison lives in Malaysia with her husband, two boys and boy/girl twins.*

JOURNAL IT

_____

What's your favorite part of the toddler years? What is the most challenging aspect of raising toddler multiples?

What do you love most about your multiples? List their individual traits.

THE MIDDLE YEARS

THE MIDDLE YEARS

MIDDLE YEARS TIPS AND ADVICE

MEGAN WOOLSEY

My triplets turned nine years old this year. Their strong-willed personalities and relentless questions often leave me breathless and exhausted. At the end of the day I often feel overwhelmed, but the joy of watching these three lovely humans move through life together makes it all worth it.

In nine years, the triplets have taught me what it means to love someone unconditionally, because they show each other that kind of love every day. This is not to say that they don't fight with each other sometimes, but in the end, all that is left is love and forgiveness. There is nothing they would not do for each other.

The middle years, those years between the ages of three and eight, can be considered the golden years of parenting. The occurrence of temper tantrums has dwindled to acceptable lows. This age group can do so much for themselves now, including tying their shoes, getting breakfast, contributing to household chores, and brushing their teeth. There are also challenges that arise: the frequency of sibling rivalry can increase; challenges navigating school with wombmates can create jealousy or competition; a lack of privacy between siblings; and food pickiness can be a big problem.

Among my triplets, two are exceptional at math and language (and school in general) while the other struggles in academics. Recently, the two triplets who perform better in school were asked to participate in an advanced language class. My heart broke for the one left behind. I fretted over the fact that she might feel she wasn't good enough, or didn't measure up to the other two. I rushed to tell her that she has so many different gifts such as horseback riding, adventure seeking, and she is the comedian of the family. But in a proud mommy moment, I realized she already knew all of this, and she felt confident in her unique abilities because I had always expressed this to her.

The lack of privacy is absolutely a fact of life in our house. Since my triplets are still all in the same class and always have been, if one of them gets in trouble or has an issue with a friend at school, the others come home and tell me about it. Of course, it is not their story to tell, but it is difficult for them not to be in every aspect of each other's business, since their lives are so intertwined.

Here are five tips to keep your sanity raising multiples during those middle years:

1. Encourage multiples to discuss issues with each other before tattling to a parent. Discuss how important it is to only involve parents with open knowledge from both or all parties.

2. Keep an open dialogue about competition and jealousy with your multiples, reassuring them that even though they were born at the same time, they still have their own special and unique personality traits and gifts.

3. Don't rush to intervene to solve all the sibling rivalry issues that may arise, or you will wind up driving yourself and your kids crazy. If they come to you with a small or medium-sized conflict, encourage them to work it out amongst themselves. It is not your job to be a constant referee. When your multiples solve their own problems, they learn valuable life lessons.

4. I know you have heard this a million times since having kids but let me reinforce the notion that you should not make special meals for the picky eater in the family. As frustrating as it may be to see one or more of your multiples turning meals away untouched, it will hurt everyone, in the long run, to cave into finicky habits. Plus, you are the parent of multiples, and you certainly don't have time for that.

5. Create a set of responsibilities for your twins, triplets, or more that will teach them the importance of contributing to the household. Mom and dad of multiples have double or triple the dishes, laundry, and picking up around the house, so it is important that you create an age-appropriate chore list for when they are three years old and up.

Cherish these years between the toddler and tween years. These are the years that your multiples are learning important life skills that will carry them through to adulthood.

A MULTIPLIED LIFE

JARED BOND

It seems obvious, even expected. When you're having multiples, many aspects of your life will be multiplied. But when you're living it, when it is your life, these exponential increases sometimes feel overwhelming.

Of course, these feelings of being overwhelmed start early. Feedings take much longer. Breaks between rest periods seem much shorter. Mere moments pass between one baby falling asleep and the next one waking.

You're in a small room at the pediatrician's office. Three babies, three adults. Two nurses bring in three trays, lined with shots, alcohol swabs, and Band-Aids. The tiny room is meant only for a few people, yet now it holds eight, and you glance nervously at the door to see if anyone else will try to cram into the room. Then the crying starts. One baby shrieking after getting stuck with a needle is enough to fray anyone's nerves. The screaming is constant, the baby turns beet red as he struggles for air between world-ending cries. But you're not done. The second child gets her shot. Then the third. The screams reverberate off the walls of the room, which feels smaller than it was moments ago. When the appointment ends, you make a mad dash for the car. The screaming follows you the whole way, as do the incredulous stares from the other parents in the waiting room.

When the kids were eight, two of the three had tonsillectomies and adenoidectomies on the same day. Many parents have had to endure the difficulty of helping their child through this painful process. It's often a ritual procedure of growing up. But fewer have had to help two of their children through the process at the same time. To see both of them helpless, in pain that you are unable to remove, drove my wife to tears. I remember in the car ride home, one of my daughters threw up. We told her, "It's okay. The doctor said you might feel better after throwing up." To which our other daughter asked, "Should I throw up, too?" We shouted, "NO!" (Probably a bit too loudly, but some things you just don't want multiplied.)

You have to really think and plan as your life becomes multiplied. Lost teeth? Find out what the going rate is for the tooth fairy, and now imagine having to pay for a dozen lost teeth in a single year. How much can your wallet take?

Piano lessons. Violin lessons. Guitar lessons. Boy Scouts. Girl Scouts. Baseball. Art classes. Any activity that is developmentally appropriate gets multiplied by three, in terms of both financial and time commitments. One elementary science fair project is difficult enough, but three due on the same day seems criminal.

Overall, though, I don't think the collective experience is that much different from that of parents of singletons. If you have three children, you go through the same ordeals. They all have to get shots. They all lose their teeth. They all complete that enormous second grade project on China. But somehow, I feel that the second, or third time around, a parent's previous experience lessens the shock. You've done this before. You've come out on the other side. But for us, for parents of a set of triplets, we don't get the benefit of the wisdom of experience. We have to go through it one time, and all at the same time. It's not just one crying baby in the room, it's three.

We know that these multiplied experiences can take a toll. There is a lot of research about the increased likelihood of divorce for parents of multiples. The stress of it all is sometimes more than a marriage can handle. But early on in our triplet pregnancy, we came across another scientific study that gave us hope. Scientists had polled families of multiples and singletons about their level of happiness. As expected, they found that parents of multiples, on a whole, were less happy than parents of singletons. However, after a certain point, they got over the initial stress of rearing multiple babies, or dealing with the terrible twos times three. Suddenly, their happiness level increased, and to a point beyond that of the average family of singletons. We kept this as our goal. We could make it over the hump. We could get to the point where the multiplication of positives outweighed the multiplication of the negatives.

Our kids became close friends as they grew older. When they were five, we started seeing the multiplied benefits of having triplets outweigh the hardships (and they started sleeping better, too). Play dates weren't needed, as they had each other to run about as a little pack of playmates. As school became more challenging, they became work buddies. Checking in on completing assignments. Reviewing material and quizzing each other in the car. They tapped into the benefits of having siblings of the same age. We could trust them on their own, because they weren't on their own – they had each other.

They worked together to make up their own plays, which they eagerly performed to willing family members. They created a book club in their tree house. They enjoyed singing, and worked together perfecting and performing various songs. Practicing individual musical instruments turned into jam sessions with a piano, violin, and guitar accompaniment.

Then there was the trip to Disney World. It was a birthday present, one last hurrah to visit the Magic Kingdom before they were too old to appreciate it any longer. We took them on their birthday, which they also share with their mother – a quadruple birthday. And like all things in a multiplied life, it required some planning to pull off the

69

perfect day. The hours of research on the Disney forums, the creation of custom birthday T-shirts, and remembering the birthday hats at the last minute – it all worked. Our family was chosen to open the park! Though they had woken up before dawn to travel to Disney World, meeting Mickey and Minnie Mouse, Elsa and Anna, Daisy Duck, and the Mayor of Main Street energized the kids as they waved to the hundreds of guests while fireworks went off behind us. This would not have happened were we not a family of multiples. Fast passes and photos provided by Disney, and all the planning made this a perfect day. Lunch at Cinderella's Castle, riding every ride in the park, and staying past the closing fireworks show exhausted all of us, but the glow we saw on the kids' faces and the multiplied happiness gave us the energy to ride the last ferry out of the park.

We had turned the corner. We had survived. And looking back, we could see so many amazing aspects of our lives that had become multiplied. The hugs, being buried under three sets of arms. The naps on the couch with multiple warm babies on your chest. The instant friends our children made with each other, knowing that whatever they were experiencing, the others were, too.

When having multiples, aspects of your life will be multiplied. And you'll be so thankful for the experience.

Before becoming a middle school English teacher, Jared Bond was a stay-at-home dad to his triplets. While he doesn't remember much about that first year, he took copious notes so that he could share the experience with other parents of multiples (and himself, once he caught up on sleep).

FIVE YEARS IN

REBECCA BORGER

They are together, side by side, flat out on their bellies. Somehow, they both fit the width of the couch. Head to head, long leg to leg, in matching skirts and tops, watching a movie on the tablet. Their shining heads bent together – one brown, one blonde, both in glasses. Even though they are fraternal, there is a hint of mirror imaging – one with a weak left eye, the other, the right. Both have to patch their opposite eyes daily. Their hair parts off center on the opposite sides of their heads.

My eyes frame their image for the album in my mind. This daily view never fails to fill my heart with astonishment and gratitude. My twins. My girls. Why such astonishment? Yes, twins are a wonder. But mine? Well, mine came after five sons; long after one lone daughter stood poised in the middle of a brotherly lineup. They came after years of wondering if there would ever be another little girl in our home. I treasure the joy of raising them. Experiencing life through their two sets of marveling, feminine eyes fills me with delight. Lately, I have begun to experience rainbows, snowflakes, and hearts of all sorts in a whole new dimension as they covet snowflake underwear, rainbow cookies, and heart bracelets. And everything times two. Always.

A famous line from Disney's Cinderella states, "A dream is a wish your heart makes ..." It is a dream come true to be a mom to my twin girls. Every year, more of the realization of this beautiful, secret dream I didn't even know I longed for unfolds. My heart swells and I, as much as I dare, soak in the joy. Like the unprecedented excitement and shrill glee of last Christmas when they participated in holiday cookie-making. Never has there been such deeply expressed delight in this house! These girls are my dream come true.

They are five. Five years of my heart burst wide open. Five years of everything in double – of crying in stereo (yes, they still do!), of teeth, and baths, and diapers, then the potty; of brushing pretty hair and shiny teeth. Five years of experiencing the impact of twins, which is exponential and continuous. It did not take me long to realize that this impact is not a hurdle to be overcome. Rather, it is a journey which continues through life. In those early days, the familiar motto, "Take it one day at a time" became my mantra. Looking too far ahead was overwhelming. As the years go by, I have found this is a precious gift. Having twins has taught me to slow down and be fully present in each moment.

Recently, I stood outside next to the swing set, keenly aware that I would not be pushing these small girls on swings for very long. Sure enough, within the month, one had learned to pump. And how high she flies! I am caught with my heart in my throat, torn between wanting to slow her down and recognizing that she is big enough to fly this high. My other wee girl has not quite mastered this skill. We have fully entered the space in life where their milestones are staggered, and they are aware of it. Often, there are tears. Some things come easily for one twin, and not the other. When this happens, I am always there with the quick reassurance and the reminder: They are their own individuals. They each have their own strengths, and they don't have to be the same or happen at the same time. And most times, the stormy emotions are settled and we continue to develop as unique people. For I grow, too, in heart and mind each year with them.

The twins celebrated their fifth birthday in July. This milestone arrived in the blink of an eye, leaving all of those sweet and challenging baby days behind. There, stretching before me, were two slender little girls. They sometimes tell me, "We're big girls now, Mommy! We're big girls!" They tell me this when they want to assure me that they are able to handle a new setting, adventure, or art supply. And big they are. Yet still small, too. I am startled by the realization that they are ready for kindergarten, for reading, for school, for new paths of independence.

Yesterday, I was sitting in a precious and familiar chair. Precious to me because we purchased it when the babies were due any day. I lumbered down the main street of our small mountain town on a quest to purchase La-Z-Boy recliners. We bought one rocker recliner and one regular recliner in matching corduroy brown. Familiar to me because I spent hours and hours in that rocker with the babies tucked under my chin and my feet pounding the floor in a tight rhythm. I slept in those chairs too, the weeks before they were born, when the heartburn fired right through me and the weight of the babies made it hard to breathe. And now, there is comfort in the contours of those chairs.

As I was sitting there, one of my little girls sidled up to me, thumb in her mouth, and blankie in hand. She murmured to me, "For hours and hours." She knew I would know just what she meant. She was reminding me of our shared memory. Just a few months ago, I pulled her to my chest and whispered a precious story to her. I told her of the hours I rocked and held her in those chairs. She giggled with delight, thrilled as my loving memory became hers. So, when she came to me murmuring "for hours and hours", we sunk into the chair together and began to rock.

Minutes later, her brown-haired sister came close and I gathered her into our embrace. I held my five-year-old darlings; my arms as full of love as they have been every day since the day of their birth. They still fit under my chin. Again, I can feel those two wee bundles, swaddled firmly and tucked up in each arm, nestled under my chin. And I, too, am comforted by the sweetness of our love. I am thankful for the riches of their double birth. They are two of the treasures of my life.

I am five years in. Five years ago, I became a twin mom and during all those long hard hours of rocking, sleep deprivation, tears, endless feeds, and diapers changes, I am determined to remember that babies don't keep. Praise be, they grow. They grow and still, in the midst of relentless changes (kindergarten?!), I am cupping the days in my open palms. Because then, as these days, years, and seasons fly by, I can be sure that I am enjoying the ride: the wind in my face, the sun in my eyes. Alive.

Rebecca Borger lives in Maryland with her husband and nine children, including five-year-old fraternal twin girls. She earned her BA in English with Writing and Education from Lehigh University in Bethlehem, Pennsylvania. After living hidden in the rural mountains of Western North Carolina for six years, her family relocated to Maryland in 2013.

SEPARATION ANXIETY

WHITNEY FLEMING

I stand to the side of the classroom door and peek in through the large rectangular window clouded with stickers of animated pencils, books, and pink erasers.

In the middle of a room, a tiny brunette sits at a table with several other girls playing a board game. Her small face beams as I watch her little hands toss dice onto the table, then move a purple piece around the board. She triumphantly throws her hands in the air, exchanges high-fives, and glows with pride. I know I will hear about her victory as soon as she gets off the bus later that day.

I scan the rest of the room and finally cast my eyes on a tiny, blonde-haired girl with gray-blue eyes sitting at a desk in a quiet corner. My other daughter tightly grips a pink crayon so hard I can see the change in color of her knuckles as she moves her hand up and down while biting her lower lip, signaling she is concentrating hard on her project.

To her right is a tow-headed boy. The two seem unaware of each other until I suddenly see his mouth move, and my daughter stops what she is doing to reach into her desk. She whips out a dark green crayon and unceremoniously hands it to the boy, who responds with a slight smile and a thumbs up.

Tears spring to my eyes watching the interaction, and then I jump as I feel a hand on my shoulder.

I whip around and lock eyes with my twin girls' first-grade teacher. Miss Moore is a lovely young woman who is chic and sophisticated, yet doesn't shy from getting her hands dirty with her students.

"I'm so sorry to keep you waiting," she exclaims quickly. As she leads me into a small room across the hall, I am surprised at the butterflies in my stomach. I know my kids are having a great year, but it is always nerve-wracking to sit down with a teacher.

"Okay," she exhales as she sits down, shuffling papers on the desk. "Let's start with Payton."

She hands me a piece of paper with a checklist of items typical first-graders should be able to do at this point in the year. I listen and nod my head accordingly as she goes through each one.

"I'm thrilled with her reading progress and her handwriting has vastly improved as well."

"She seems to have a real aptitude for math, so we should make sure to look for opportunities to challenge her further."

"Yes, she's a little competitive, but she keeps it in check most of the time."

There is nothing surprising about this conversation, nothing out of place. My "Twin A" loves school. She loves everything. Life comes easy for this tiny human, and she attacks it with vim and vigor.

"Okay, moving on. I can't wait to show you some of Olivia's work," she says excitedly.

My heart starts beating a little faster, and the room feels warm. I try listening to my daughters' teacher as she shows me a few of her math papers, but instead, some other memories pop into my head.

"She will most likely have learning problems like dyslexia."

"We are hopeful that she may live a normal life."

"You need to prepare yourself for a long road ahead."

These aren't snippets from teachers' reports; instead, they are prognoses from a slew of medical experts about my daughter when we weren't sure how to help her as a struggling toddler with significant developmental delays.

Her symptoms were confusing. She walked early at 11 months, but immediately started moving high up on her toes, like a ballerina. She could recite verses from songs and recognize letters, but couldn't ask for "more milk." She bonded deeply with her family and therapists, but did not have an interest in other children.

Doctors could not pinpoint what was wrong with her, and we received a variety of misdiagnoses: apraxia, dyspraxia, Sensory Processing Disorder, PDD-NOS, Asperger's. The list was long, yet never seemed to fit.

When she was nearly five, we saw an orthopedic surgeon to assess her toe-walking since therapy was not helping. We were shocked when the doctor told us our daughter had a minor case of cerebral palsy (CP). In his opinion, although it did not show up on her MRI, she had experienced trauma in the womb that caused a neurological issue, forcing her lower leg muscles to function improperly and interrupting communication between the brain and other regions of her body. This, coupled with some tight tendons, caused her to be a constant, extreme toe-walker. He also explained that the toe-walking had a significant impact on her developmental progress.

"Could you imagine trying to spend your life balanced on your tippy toes, then process information?" he asked us.

While the news was a shock, I was relieved at the same time. The peg finally fit in the hole. CP often causes issues with speech and fine motor skills, but it was non-progressive, which is why we were seeing her developmental skills improve, albeit slowly.

We decided to aggressively pursue treatment for my daughter's physical condition, which seemed to be a major issue for her both in developing motor skills and her confidence. The doctor would cut her Achilles' tendons, elongate them, and then reattach them to allow her to walk on her flat feet without pain. It was bittersweet when the doctor came out to tell us that she had one of the most severe cases he had ever seen, but the surgery was successful.

Immediately after, she began to flourish in leaps and bounds. With a more centered core, it was easier for her to find words and process information for conversation. Her spatial awareness improved. Her sensory needs reduced, and she expressed a desire to learn to read. She became more confident and easier to deal with, since she could now communicate her wants and needs.

On her first day of kindergarten, she walked through the doors on her flat feet, without an aide, and with her twin sister by her side. Although she was still behind her peer group and required additional support in a few areas, she surpassed all expectations.

It was a simple decision to keep our girls together. Olivia's communication and social skills were limited, and we felt better knowing Payton would be there to help her make friends or reduce the chances of bullying. The two played well together, and we did not anticipate any problems in the classroom. While we always treated them as individuals at home, we also knew that they would thrive in different activities if they had the option of doing it together.

My thoughts are interrupted when my daughters' teacher grabs my arm and says, "Check this out! She did this one hundred percent on her own!"

She shows me a picture of what I guess is a palm tree with Christmas balls hanging from it. Underneath in dark lead handwriting, it says: "My favrit book is chika chika bom bom."

I lock eyes with her and see a mirrored reflection of pride and tears. My daughter, who often refused to draw a picture and could not write words within a line, did both. On her own. It felt like she just discovered a new planet.

I cautiously say, "I know I'm not supposed to ask, but how does she stack up to the other students? Can she hold her own?"

Her smile widens. "Not only is she holding her own, but I'd say she is in the top half of the class in math and reading." The meeting went so well I couldn't remember why I was nervous, and I couldn't wait to relay the entire conversation to my husband. Just as I was starting to thank her, Miss Moore chimed, "Well, there is one more thing I wanted to discuss with you. Have you thought about if you are going to separate the girls next year in second grade?"

I was surprised at her suggestion. The fact was I did not plan on it. That both girls just received glowing reports shoved the idea to the back of my brain. I also selfishly enjoyed them sharing a classroom and the ease of only having one classroom to track.

I thought about her comment and felt perplexed. I had one daughter who would tell me about her day from start to end, and another who barely said a word. I gave birth to one child who was an extreme extrovert and another who preferred her solitude. I felt the two were yin and yang, complementing each other where the other fell short.

My husband and I felt that as long as our girls were in a classroom together, neither would feel alone. Except, what we really meant was Olivia would never be alone.

"Well, my plan was to keep them together, but, um, what do you think?"

"Well, Olivia is doing great, I mean, really great. But I don't think she realizes how well she is doing as it's never as good as Payton. When you have a sister that always finishes first, or gets a hundred on every test, your best doesn't always seem as good."

"Did Olivia tell you this?"

"No, but I can see it when I hand back papers sometimes. She looks at her sister's grades when they put it in their folders or mailboxes, but doesn't seem to care about anyone else's scores."

"Oh, I had no idea," I respond sadly. My husband and I thought we were doing our daughter a favor, and never imagined she would get discouraged. "I think I'll talk to my husband about it. And Olivia."

The thought of separating my twins turned my stomach. How would we know if something happened to her in class? What if she was picked on or bullied? Would she be able to operate as well in the classroom without her sister?

I also contemplated the opposite. What if keeping Olivia in class with her twin was holding her back from even more progress? What did it mean for Payton to feel responsible for her sister? What benefited me and what would benefit them?

Were they stronger together or apart?

If separated, both girls would have to work on opening up, making contact, and finding ways to connect with other kids to make friends. This competence doesn't come as naturally to Olivia as it does to her sister, but both needed the opportunity to strengthen this important life skill.

Additionally, now that Olivia was finding her self-confidence, I did not want her to predetermine her destiny by labeling herself as not the 'smart one' or 'athletic one.' She needed the opportunity to find out what made her special, as opposed to being special solely because she is a twin.

Later that day, after my girls jumped off the bus, I sat them down for a talk over a snack and a glass of milk. "What if you guys were in different classrooms next year for second grade? What do you think about that?"

I was surprised when my quiet, speech-delayed daughter spoke right up and replied, "I think it's a good idea. But we'll still get to share a room though, right?"

Surprisingly, it was the alpha female who looked sad. "But I'll miss Olivia," Payton shouted, near tears.

"You'll still see her all the time, honey. And you'll appreciate each other even more if you don't see her for 24 hours a day, seven days a week."

80

"Okay then. I'll do it," she said bravely.

And the girls never looked back.

I believe separating them at school made their bond closer by eliminating any classroom competition or jealousy. They share a group of friends and take an interest in what each is working on at school. They often study side by side. They have developed more compassion for each other's shortcomings and a deeper appreciation for being a twin.

I knew I made the right decision when they brought their first vocabulary test home on the same day and saw that they both missed the exact same question, even selecting the same wrong answer. They might be in different classrooms, but their connection would not be severed.

The separation was harder on me, however. The beginning of school was torture knowing it was the first time they were not together. We faced times when one daughter was invited to a birthday party while the other felt left out. I worried that the girls did not feel I spent equal time with them at school when I had more volunteer opportunities with one classroom than another. And sometimes the wrong kid brought her library book when she should have been wearing her gym shoes.

I'm thankful to the teacher who pointed out what my husband and I couldn't see. Our emotions clouded our judgment, and our fears limited their potential.

There is no one-size-fits-all solution when it comes to separating twins. It is important to listen to teachers, your kids, and most importantly, your heart.

Whitney Fleming is a communications consultant and freelance writer living in the suburbs of Chicago. She is the mother to three active tween girls, including a set of fraternal twins. She blogs about parenting, relationships and w(h)ine.

THE MIDDLE YEARS

WALKS WITH MOM

KARI LUTES

My mom loves to walk. When she's frustrated, the only way she can shake off her mood is by 'stomping it out' on a four-mile walk through the park. She even makes her username on most websites 'Walkinlady,' a testament to her hobby. From the time I was in my mother's womb, I was walking with her. She'd push my brother in a stroller as she walked to keep herself healthy during her pregnancy. When we were babies, my mom put my twin sister and me in a stroller every evening and set out around our neighborhood to sell Avon. She even made friends with neighbors because of the conversations started about her twin baby girls. By the age of six, I was known as Mom's 'walking buddy.' Wherever Mom went, I was ready to go with her, and she was happy to have me along, though it meant slower and shorter walks for her.

I looked forward to our walks in the evenings, eager to share the stories of my day at school. Sometimes, Mom and I walked to a Kmart a mile from our home. We'd set out from our cul-de-sac, passing the stop sign that usually marked my boundaries, traipsing down the hill to the row of houses at the front of the neighborhood. Once we left the neighborhood, the straight sidewalks disappeared and we balanced between the side of the road and strangers' front yards. With my mom walking between me and the traffic, I chattered happily, anticipating reaching Kmart and selecting a piece of candy as my fuel for the walk back home.

We always walked after dinner. This evening hour, as the sun set in the pinks of the Kentucky sky, was my time to be with Mom. The one time in my day when I was just Kari—not one of the twins. After putting on my shoes, I'd wait by the garage for my mom while she put in another load of laundry before heading outside to join me. One day, my twin sister, Kayla, followed me outside.

I tried to keep my gaze from meeting hers. Though I noticed the Skechers on her feet, I refused to acknowledge what I knew she wanted. I turned away from her, heading into the garage. She was going to make me an *and* during my time to be a *me*.

"Kari?" She followed me in.

My fingers glided along the top of my silver scooter, and I ignored her.

"Do you mind if I come with you?"

I considered nodding as I turned to face her.

"You *are* Mom's walking buddy, so I won't go if you don't want me to." Her brown eyes met mine. "I really want to come."

"You can't." My eyes narrowed at her, and I stepped out of the garage as I saw my mom approaching.

"Okay," Kayla sighed, turning to go. She, too, knew the cost of *and.*

Mom was stepping up to us, walking shorts on and white tennis shoes laced on her feet. "Are you coming with us today, Kayla?"

My twin looked back at me before shaking her head at Mom. "No, I'm not."

My walk with Mom was different that night. I didn't chatter by her side. I feared if I did, my words would become my confession. I didn't want to be sorry. I wanted to be with my mom. But in keeping my sister from my mom, I realized I'd distanced myself from her as well. Mom loved us both, and she wanted to spend the precious moments with us both—I was the only one keeping us from being together, as we had been before Kayla and I had even entered this world.

When the walk was over, I lacked the special feeling of being known and enjoyed by my mom; instead, I felt wretched. I hurried inside, kicking off my shoes by the front door before peeking into the living room and spying my sister sitting on our blue velvet couch. I approached her shyly, climbing onto the couch beside her. She turned to me, the sadness in her eyes the only indication of our conversation before my walk with Mom.

"How was your walk?"

I sighed, looking down at the golden toes of my socks. "It was okay." My arms wrapped around my knees, and I glanced up at my sister. "You can come next time if you want."

Kayla brightened, her attention no longer split between me and the T.V. screen. "Really?" Her voice dropped. "But you're Mom's walking buddy—are you sure?"

I nodded, letting go of the title and embracing the *and*. Kari and Kayla would be Mom's walking buddy, not just Kari.

"I'm sure," I said. "I like to walk with you, too."

As the third child of four and with the added cloak of being a twin, I'd always felt I went by unnoticed. When people, especially relatives, talked to me and my sister, they would direct a single question to both of us. Somehow, Kayla always answered first, and once they had her answer, no one ever waited for mine. Once, when my grandma called me "Kayla" by mistake, and my dad corrected her, she responded, "Close enough." Instances like this had taught me that the best way to be known was to separate myself from my twin. I'd thought that by denying my sister a share in the precious moments with our mom, I would be able to keep them grasped tightly in my fist. I realized that by keeping her from our mom's presence, I was actually keeping myself from Mom, too. By clinging so tightly to my identity as

Mom's 'walking buddy', I kept myself from being known in other ways to her and being known by my sister.

Since then, walks with Kayla and Mom have morphed into more walks with Kayla than with Mom. As we grew older, conversations together were more desired than time with Mom. We moved from our neighborhood to a house with six acres. Along the creek at the front of the yard, Kayla and I have carved a path beneath the trees, a testament to hours spent in each other's company planning novels or trying to determine what we will be in the world.

Occasionally, I walk with just Mom. Mom doesn't like to walk in the yard, so we usually walk in a neighborhood close to home, as we have since the beginning. Sometimes I even ask Kayla if she wants to walk alone with Mom, and she still checks with me. Usually if one of us says yes, the other understands. No matter how old we get, some days it's still special to walk with Mom.

Kari Lutes is a twin turned writer through the detailed, imaginative games she played with her twin sister, Kayla. Kari is a senior creative writing and English major at Asbury University in Wilmore, Kentucky.

EVERYONE WAS RIGHT

MEGAN WOOLSEY

When the triplets were babies and I was brave enough to take them out into the world, the spectacle of three babies in a triple stroller and a tired mom in yoga pants wearing a fake smile was just too much to resist. Strangers would approach us and ask if they were triplets and then offer words of wisdom, or express just how sorry they felt for me.

On one of those rare moments when I decided to brave the world with one-year-old triplets in tow, I encountered a mom who stopped me outside of Starbucks to ask if they were triplets. Why yes, they are, I said, gearing up for responses that ranged from, "You are blessed" to "If it were me, I would die!" Instead, she told me that she has triplets and they are in high school now. She told me that I am in the trenches right now since they are so young, but good times await me. She offered to have her triplets babysit mine, and I could tell she genuinely wanted to help me. She was one of the rare people who really understood what I was going through. I generally received one of two kinds of enlightenment from moms and dads of twins, triplets and more, as they would glance at my infants and think to themselves, "I'm sure as hell glad we aren't in *that* place anymore."

"Just wait until they are five years old because that is when EVERYTHING gets easier."

"It never gets easier. Every phase is difficult, but the difficulty in raising multiples just evolves as the years progress."

Whenever anyone told me that in five years my life was going to be golden, I imagined myself sipping my glass of champagne by the pool while my triplets plus one played peacefully for hours on end. In five years, all my hard labor and sleepless nights would be rewarded. This is exactly what I wanted people to tell me! This is what I wanted to hear. How did they know? They knew because they were me once and that is what they hoped someone would tell them. These were the powerful, merciful people with whom I crossed paths early on.

The moms and dads of multiples who told me that it would essentially never get easier left me feeling that my life was doomed. I imagined a lifetime of absurd meltdowns and demands that would require 24-hour mental and physical exertion, leaving me with premature gray hair and a permanent resting bitch face (RBF).

I always held tight to the notion that five would be the magical age of peace and harmony in my house; a time we would finally be able to sit around a dinner table and the triplets would eat any combination of food I served them without complaint, and then they would do all the dishes while I binge-watched Dateline and ate M&Ms with reckless abandon.

My triplets are now nine years old and here is what I know: everyone was right. It did get easier when the triplets were five because I wasn't cleaning shitty diapers and wiping spit-up off my shirt all hours of the day. I wasn't hauling a 40-pound car seat in the crook of each arm (yes massage therapist, that is why I have a trillion knots in my shoulders) or waking up three different times at night to breastfeed one baby with my left boob and bottle-feed the other baby with my right hand, simultaneously (and if Daddy wasn't home to help, well, then that third baby better just get their patient on).

By the time they were five, I was no longer chasing four kids around the park, telling them not to push others down the slide or triplet gang up on innocent singletons in the sandbox. Instead, I had other challenges that were far more emotionally taxing. The physical labor at the work camp inside my home had ended, and a new era of emotional persecution had begun. The triplets had stopped waterboarding Chris and me, so to speak, and had moved on to more devious means of torture: verbal manipulation and sibling rivalry.

At five years old, my triplets and their older sister went from a strong united front that could only be compared to The Partridge Family (loving and kind to each other) meets The Sopranos (tied together in a don't-mess-with-us mob situation), to The Lord of the Flies. The Lord of the Flies does seem like an extreme analogy, because my kids never beat each other to death, but they did begin to turn against each other in four separate plays for power, ultimate anarchy, and rule over our small island.

All of a sudden, nobody was allowed to look at the other person the wrong way; the wrong way being determined by the mood and relationship between the kids at that particular moment. After the age of five, they were all extremely verbal, and would talk over each other all day, voices becoming louder and more frustrated as they would attempt to one-up each other with their stories. During the summer when they were outdoors I would worry that the entire neighborhood was hearing their loud altercations, so I texted my friend Lea next door to suggest she shut the windows and turn on some music. She would always politely say, "I don't hear anything," because she loves me.

I was beginning to miss the days when they were toddlers and would resolve problems with a swift push to the ground or a firm bite to the arm (the teeth marks were never permanent). There was a little crying and then it was over in a minute. Now when there is an argument, there are a lot of words spoken REALLY LOUDLY and it doesn't stop for what feels like the length of time it would take to get through the movie *Space Odyssey*, twice.

Sometimes I play referee, trying to be the adult mom and find a mature conclusion to the dramatic circumstances of why one child doesn't want to be the lion, they want to be the wolf, in their imaginary play world. Other times I act like I am also a child: I scream and shout and become really unreasonable. When I am absurdly over life, I close my bedroom door and turn on a T.V. show just loud enough that I don't have to hear the bickering. I can't say that any of my tactics are better than the other for handling the multiples mayhem, because they all have their rightful place in my arsenal of survival tactics.

I am painting a bleak picture of what it is like to have triplets, and that isn't altogether fair. The past nine years hasn't been all physical and emotional pain. While it's true that some nights I may indulge in just one more glass of wine to take the edge off, I have never spent any time in a psych ward, so how hard can it be? I'm sure it's not openly discussed in social settings or Internet groups, but I don't hear of too many parents of multiples losing their minds merely because they are raising multiples, so that's good.

At nine years old, my triplets are the best of friends. When they watch a movie, they sit so close to each other, they are practically in each other's laps. When they play together, sometimes they fight, but mostly they laugh. The other day my triplet son fell off the monkey bars at school and hurt the side of his face. He was crying. His sisters escorted him up to the school office and they were crying right along with him. They refused to leave his side. The school receptionist called me and said that the triplets are in the office, one is hurt and the other two are by his side in support and solidarity. It is just so sweet, she said. She hadn't ever seen anything like it.

They are still all in the same classroom at school. They have been in the same class forever. I told them that next year they should all have their own classrooms so they can create some independence from each other and make their own friends. They all wholeheartedly refuse to be separated from each other.

When they were babies, Chris and I took them to the mall so we could look like a circus act and have a lot of people stare and gawk at us. A group of three elderly people, one man and two women, approached us to tell us that they were also triplets. We are never apart, they told us. Even in their 80s they shop at the mall together. As they walked away, there was barely an inch to spare between each of them as they shuffled across the tile floors. I imagine that will be my triplets when they are in their 80s.

Moms and dads of multiples learn quickly what it means to be strong and how we find this strength in the love we have, being fortunate enough to parent multiples. When people ask me if it is easier now that they are nine years old, I say no. No, it's not easier, but it's not harder. Sometimes it's stressful, other times it's blissful. Sometimes raising multiples has me laughing, other times I cry. Raising multiples runs the entire gamut of emotions in one day. For moms and dads of multiples, the only constant that we can count on is that some days are fun, and some days are hard, and absolutely everything comes in multiples.

Megan Woolsey is a writer living in California with her supportive husband, a set of triplets, and their big sister. Megan is published in many national publications, and is an essayist in two anthologies. For a list of her work, go to MeganWoolsey.com.

"MOMMY, I WANT TO BE WITH MY BROTHER"

SHELLEY STOLAROFF SEGAL

My dreams exploded like firecrackers when Josh and Jordan were born in 1996. My expectations were unchecked. My little boy and girl would make me chuckle with their twin-speak. They would crawl together, laugh together, plot together. They would compete athletically, and academically, but never spiritually. Their bond would launch them on a shared trajectory, and they would love and support each other throughout their lives. Their connection was real, and they would never be separated.

Three years later when Josh was diagnosed with severe autism, my dreams vanished as quickly as they had exploded, and my expectations dipped below an invisible nadir. My toddler lost all of his speech as well as other key functions. His autism was insidious, spreading over him like a shadow – but it never passed. And when the behaviors and medical problems fully took hold, Jordan became confused about her twin brother. Sometimes his eyes would lock with hers in a soulful, transcendent way, and sometimes he just didn't see her at all. His disengagement and aggression troubled me, and I worried about my daughter. But she was loyal to him. She prided herself on being his "therypist." "It's good that I talk a lot, Mommy, because Joshie can hear my words." I wish it hadn't been necessary to separate them because of his therapies, but I didn't have a choice. I got used to hearing, "I want my brother to go with me to my school. My teachers can teach him!"

When the kids turned five, my husband and I had to make a decision about our son. He was exhausted all the time. I remember putting him in a plastic pool outside just to keep him awake for his table work. Jeff is a former neurosurgeon. He always suspected Josh was having seizures, even though his EEGs were consistently negative. We finally ended up taking him to Houston for an advanced test, and this time the results were positive. He was having nocturnal seizures, some lasting as long as 20 minutes, which explained the chronic fatigue and brain fog. Jeff said we should operate as soon as possible.

Typically, when we flew Josh around the country to see specialists, we returned home swiftly to keep things 'normal.' But in 2002, only one hospital in the country performed the bilateral MST procedure Josh needed, and it was in Omaha. We would be there for almost a month, because the procedure required three different operations. I was terrified about my son having brain surgery, but the idea of separating my twins for a month rattled me almost as much.

But we had no choice. We sent Jordan to Texas to be with her grandparents and cousins. It was a sensible idea, and we were grateful to Jeff's parents for taking her. Protecting my daughter from potential trauma was wise, wasn't it? I recorded the following in my journal: "We must be away for a month. I must leave my sweet Jordan. She will fly to Texas and go to school with her cousins. Anxiety I can taste in my mouth. Metallic. "You get to go to Texas! Lucky, lucky girl!" "Mommy, I want to be with my brother! I want to help you!" Anxiety that seeps through my clothes. She sniffs my fear. "Mommy, why do you have to go? Why can't Daddy fix Joshie's brain?" I want to take her with me. I need her and she needs to be with her brother. What if we've made a mistake? What if something happens to him on the table? Thank God Mom's coming with me."

94

Four weeks and three agonizing operations later, my son was sitting in his hospital bed in Nebraska doing wooden puzzles. He pulled through the surgeries better than I did. And when we spoke to Jordan in Texas, she was happy. She never stopped asking about Josh, though, and could barely wait for our reunion at the airport.

He was alert and sitting in a wheelchair. I'll never forget how she handled the sight of her brother after his surgeries. He wouldn't keep his cloth cap on and his swollen head looked like a bloody baseball. He'd also lost weight. When Jordan ran to greet him, her mouth flew open and she cried a little. She wasn't scared, though, just sad. "Joshie, let me hold your hand. Let me make you feel better!" She gripped him as we wheeled him through the airport. Two parts, one whole.

I learned never to separate the kids again when I discovered that Jordan wasn't frightened of anything medical or anything Josh. Shortly after we returned, we had to drain spinal fluid from his head. It was necessary to put restraints on him and pin him down while the doctor inserted a large needle to extract the fluid. We didn't want Jordan to see this so we put her in another room down the hall. Josh's nightmarish screams were expected and familiar, but Jordan's shrieks were sickening. How ignorant of me in hindsight to 'protect' her from the situation. She was desperate to participate. She kept wailing from the other room, "I want to help you! I want to be with my brother! Mommy, I want to be with my brother!" She wasn't put off by his screams, only the pain creating them.

Throughout the years, Jordan assisted me in blood draws, transfusions, and the administration of meds. She has helped me with Josh's seizures, falls, and hospitalizations. She signed with him when they were little, and created computer programs aimed at his academic success. She wanted to be an integral part of his physical and mental recovery.

She still does. And Josh loves his "Sissy" and senses her devotion. Jordan's four-year-old words were prophetic when she whispered them in her brother's ear so many years ago. He was getting a blood draw from his foot. "Joshie, please don't cry. Just hold my hand Joshie, just squeeze it when it's bad. I love you Josh. I will love you and take care of you forever." Nothing will break that connection. Their special bond has exceeded my wildest dreams.

Shelley Stolaroff Segal is a playwright, performer, and essayist living in Greensboro, NC. My Son, *her play about autism and race, premiered in NYC and was presented at TEDx East. Her non-fiction credits include* The Washington Post, Blunt Moms, Voices from the Spectrum, Chicken Soup for the Soul, Multiples Illuminated, *and* From Sac Literary Journal. *In addition to creating an album of children's music, she's been working on the same book for six years now and is hoping it will literally write itself one day.*

THREE'S A CROWD

GINA GRANTER

"Please come collect your children. It is impossible for us to supervise them together."

It was before noon on the first day of a summer dance camp, and already I was being asked to retrieve my twin girls. This was not surprising to me: I knew to be especially attentive to my phone the first time anyone was in charge of the two of them. In swim class, the teacher said we'd need to put them in separate groups: there was no way to teach them together, and their antics made them a drowning hazard. In ballet, the teachers instituted a rule of two children between them at all times, and appeared relieved to hear I would not be enrolling the twins in the next session.

At school, they are in separate classes, and no longer able to meet at the schoolyard during playtimes. They had to be separated because of "*chicanerie toujours ensemble*," or "chicanery together, always." Maybe that will be the name of their future punk band. Or their anarchist revolution.

It's hard to imagine that I was once living a peaceful, studious, child-free life, where chaos felt more within my control, and headaches were caused by a crazy night out, not crazy twin girls. Wrapping up my PhD coursework in the small city of St. John's, Newfoundland, I was 27 and desperate to return to Montreal. Occasional weekends in Toronto for my part-time job were, in the meantime, opportunities for indulgence in everything a big city had to offer.

One weekend of such indulgence led me to my first pregnancy test. Two clear lines emerged instantly. The guy wanted nothing to do with me. I was okay doing this myself. Friends were shocked by the news that I was going to have a baby; I was pro-choice, loved martinis and late nights, and had a promising academic career. But this was going to be a turning point for me. I envisioned myself traveling the world with my baby cozied up against my chest. I'd write as he slept. We'd move as a unit. It would be us against the world. We'd show everyone we needed no pity. I was going to have someone who loved me back the way that I loved, and oh, would I love this child.

Twenty weeks into my pregnancy, back in Montreal, I had my first ultrasound. When the technician put the wand on my belly, I instantly saw two round shapes. Two heads. Two babies.

All the images I'd held in my mind of me moving about my life with a child attached to my chest suddenly disappeared. I looked at my friend who'd accompanied me to the appointment. He stared at the monitor in awe, beaming. I resolved to take his expression as a guide to how I should feel about this new development.

I had to change doctors and was referred to an obstetrician who specialized in high-risk pregnancies. I was advised that I should avoid orgasms and take other measures to minimize the risk of premature birth. Despite my not having a partner, this was difficult because I was watching the entire series of *The Sopranos* and had a profound crush on James Gandolfini. But I persevered.

The twins were due in December. By September, strangers were asking me why I wasn't already in the hospital. In October, a woman pointed to my belly on the bus and exclaimed, "Two girls! Scorpios!" Twins are full term at 36 weeks. Usually doctors intervene at 38 weeks. Mine stayed cozily inside me until 39 weeks, when labor was induced, and I gave birth, nearly 20 hours later, to two 7-pound, healthy baby girls. Sagittarians.

The day we came home from the hospital, I put both swaddled bundles next to each other in the same crib, which they'd share for the first four months, to help regulate their heartbeats: standard practice with twins. It appeared they needed proximity to each other more than they needed proximity to me. Breastfeeding was a trial, and I never had enough for them; they self-weaned in their first year after months of preferring the bottle. Their primary bond was, and always will be, with each other.

It wasn't that I didn't bond with my babies; what I remember of their infancy and early childhood is wonderful. I amazed myself with what I was capable of. My pediatrician said I should write a book about twins. They ate well, slept well, and were healthy. I sang gentle folk songs to them and said "I love you" many times each day. I didn't have to answer to anyone else's ideas about how to raise them. I traversed Montreal with my double stroller, leaving the house at 8:00 a.m. and not returning until dinner time. They napped while I walked up Mount Royal. We'd lie on blankets and eat fresh strawberries from Jean-Talon Market. They napped while I ran home. I knew I was lucky; I know I am lucky. I look at their photographs and see the attention I took not just to capture their images together, but also to get individual portraits of them. What I don't see: myself behind the camera, often forgetting to put myself in the picture, and not having someone there to invite me in.

While to me they always looked different from each other, nobody else can reliably identify them, so I have always dressed them differently to honor their individuality. On their first day of school, I took a picture of them, and when they looked at it, one of them said, "Aw, I'm so cute! Which one is me?" Neither they nor any of their teachers followed the cues of different haircuts, outfits, and the pink versus purple Chuck Taylors: everyone but me sees only similarity.

Here's the thing about twins: almost all the fun stuff about them, is only fun if you're a twin. If you're the one who needs to wrangle them into some semblance of acceptable behavior, it is constant bubble-bursting. No matter how much space they have, they end up entwined. The younger (by one minute) recently said: "It would be cool if we could get tangled up in a ball, and never separate." I can't imagine loving anyone enough to want that.

Their obsessive physicality challenges the most patient of caregivers. I insisted they go in different classes when they started school. The administration laughed but complied, yet assigned my daughters hooks next to each other in the coat room. The next week, the hooks were on opposite sides of the room. The following week, they were assigned different coat rooms. Their separate teachers reported that alone they are creative, affectionate, bright, kind children, but "We just can't get them to focus on anything when they're together."

We went through a rigorous application process to get them into a Waldorf school. I am not one for labels on types of parenting or education, and am generally against the idea of private school, but was willing to try anything to mellow the twins out a bit. Everything went superbly in the individual interviews. Then it was time for them to attend the school for three days. There was only one classroom for grade two. At pickup on the second day, we were asked to not bring them back. They hadn't done anything bad: they were just being goofballs, impossible to rein in.

Now, at age eight, they combine to become my personal Tasmanian Devil, whirling and chattering, orbiting me on the sidewalk, crossing the street without paying attention. I dread that inevitable moment when a game turns to conflict, when they turn to me suddenly, needing an ally against the other. I refuse to take sides, and they reunite in their frustration with me. At the end of each day, my patience is used up from keeping them alive and uninjured.

In recent years, I've had some relief: by the time the twins started school, their father had gotten more involved, moved to Montreal, and had partial custody of them. Their first nights away from me were agonizingly peaceful, their closed bedroom door a feeble attempt to keep me from obsessing over their empty beds. I quickly learned to adjust by maximizing the fun during my newfound freedom. The first time they spent a week away from me, I flew to Austin, Texas, for live music and dive-bar drinking. Two years ago, after dropping the kids off with their father, I flew to New York City for a comedy show, and on the train home I met the sweetest, kindest man, who is now, miraculously, my partner. The twins' time with their father enables me to have a life beyond them, maintaining a relationship with my astonishingly unflappable New Yorker, who has committed to me even though he's fully aware of the craziness of my life. He calls it 'charm.' His living in another country probably helps.

The time came for the twins to visit New York with me for the first time. The older twin had fantasies of climbing the Statue of Liberty and looking out from the crown, but that required months of advanced booking, so glimpsing Lady Liberty from the free Staten Island Ferry was going to have to do. Sensing I needed a break from their already-manic-now-charged-by-Manhattan energy, my boyfriend agreed to keep an eye on the twins while I walked around. When I returned, they were playing limbo with two ropes on the back of the ferry designed to keep passengers from falling into open water. I pleaded with them to stop. I demanded they stop. They were oblivious to anyone else's existence or to any danger. The ends of their long red hair flicked in the sunlight like the outer edges of a flame; their green eyes sparkled with exuberance. I watched as the personification of my own recklessness in conceiving them danced precariously close to launching themselves off the ferry, to certain death. Two staff members in reflective safety vests looked on, beaming. They were entertained: mesmerized, even, by the beautiful co-conspirators. The cadence of my daughters' giggles became the arrhythmia of my heartbeat: they know the power they wield, that their lookalike beauty and their built-in accomplice make them feel invincible. I am left to bear the brunt of the stress of their mutual enchantment.

On the crowded 6 train home, exhausted, I feared a mariachi band would board and amplify the twins' energy to unprecedented levels. Instead, an elderly woman made her way slowly through the train toward us, singing, her hand held out. She sang with conviction, and I recognized the song instantly: Whitney Houston's "Greatest Love of All." Her voice was weakened by age but still beautiful; it put into high relief the song's message of self-empowerment. I looked at my daughters, fearing they'd ruin the moment, interpreting "They can't take away my dignity" as a challenge. Instead, their eyes were wide open, rapt with the singer. As the woman sang the words, "I believe that children are our future," my daughters looked the part: innocence and wonder to take inspiration from. The enchantresses became the enchanted: silent, still, and spellbound. Relief washed over me as I felt, for once, like I was a part of, rather than apart from, the sort of magic that constantly hums between them.

Gina Granter teaches English at Dawson College in Montreal, where she lives with her three daughters. She is a storyteller, an occasional stand-up comedian, and an annual seamstress of Halloween costumes. She divides her time between Montreal and New York City.

A TWIN THING

AMY KESTENBAUM

"Shut up!"
"No, *you* shut up!"
"Get out of my room!"
"I hate you!"
I bury my face in my hands. I try taking deep breaths. I try tuning it out. My twin boys' bickering and epic physical fights have been constant since they burst into our lives eight years ago. By far, this has been my most difficult struggle with having twins – harder than sleepless nights, or sleep training, or potty training, or any number of more obvious parenting challenges.

I understand sibling rivalry. My twins are the middle two in a family of four children. I grew up with a brother I often had a love/hate relationship with. I understand arguing and bickering, jockeying for parents' attention, even the sibling fights that seem to arise purely out of boredom. But the discord between my twins seems to transcend anything I have ever seen between siblings. It truly is analogous to a bad marriage – one in which both spouses resent the other but can't seem to bring themselves to separate from one another.

Before having my own twins, I always imagined the twin relationship to be this amazing bond. A built-in best friend. No need for play dates, because they would have each other. I wanted them to have '*a twin thing.*' From the moment my twins could scoot and crawl, they would move toward one another and reach out for each other ... so that they could hit, scratch, or pull hair. Surely, they will become playmates when they are more verbal, I assumed. The fighting only escalated. They will start school and appreciate having one another there, I told myself. Their first preschool teacher told me to never put them in the same class ever again.

I have worried myself sick over this issue. While most articles about parenting twins stress the importance of making sure the children have their own identities, and do not depend too much on one another for socializing, I feel alone with my opposite concerns. What if they grow up and still hate each other? What if they aren't there for each other in their times of need? *Why aren't they fitting the storybook ideal I have for how twins should be?*

I know there is nothing wrong with my twins. Each of them has a strong and loving relationship with the other two children in our family. I even catch moments of true affection between the two of them: they stand up for one another on the playground at school; they come to each other's defense when one is in trouble with me or my husband; and if one is sick or injured, the other one is genuinely concerned for his brother (unless, of course, he caused the injury, in which case he is concerned for himself).

About two years ago, my husband and I decided our dysfunctional twins needed a 'divorce.' They had been sharing a bedroom since they were born. We had the space to give them each their own room, so we decided to go for it. We thought that having their own spaces in the house would help them get along better. They were excited and embraced the move. They enthusiastically packed up their belongings, dividing shared items like board games and books 50-50 (this was, after all, an amicable breakup). They happily anticipated being able to go to sleep at night and wake up in the morning without the other one *right there*.

But once they each had their own room, we noticed an interesting phenomenon. When we went to check on them after they had been put to sleep, we would frequently find them snuggled in one bed together. It was never something that was spoken about, it just would happen – and still happens from time to time. Somehow, they were drawn to one another – inexplicably, maybe even involuntarily. Perhaps they really did have the 'twin bond' I had imagined they would have. For those brief hours in the night, they were comforted by one another's presence and they were at peace together. Of course, the moment they opened their eyes, it was back to yelling and hitting, resentment and irritation. However, every day, the first thing either boy does when he wakes up is go into his twin's room. It might be to argue, but they still seek that initial connection to start the day with each other – not their other siblings, nor their parents.

I can't begin to understand what pulls them toward one another at night, and what drives such a wedge between them during the day. I have to believe it is one and the same force pushing them in both directions. Perhaps I don't understand because I'm not a twin. Maybe what defines their relationship is the sheer intensity of their feelings toward one another – positive and negative, conscious, and even subconscious. Perhaps this incredibly strong reaction to one another is their own unique *twin thing* that I have been searching for this whole time.

Amy Kestenbaum lives in Los Angeles with her four children ages 4-10 (including twin boys, age 8) and her husband, Mark. Originally from Chicago, Amy graduated from Emory University and UCLA School of Law. In the rare moments when she's not in carpool lines, Amy holds leadership positions in several nonprofit organizations in her community.

HE GOT MORE: THE EPIC BATTLE ON THE TWINSHIP

PAMELA ALMA WEYMOUTH

"He's taking three! He already had two! Maaaaama!" Aidan is screaming loud enough that they can probably hear him in Tibet. On a daily basis, the possibility of the walls crumbling due to the injustices of twinship feels like a real threat.

Quinn is plunging the stainless ladle in for his third helping of butternut squash ravioli—my favorite six-minute meal. His bowl is piled so high it's unlikely that he will eat all five hundred squares, but he's starving, dinner is late, and his avarice is less about hunger than about the fact that if he doesn't get that extra scoop, his brother might get more.

This is the same argument my sons have had since the day they were born. No matter how many times I try to reassure them that there's enough food in the house, enough money in the bank, enough space on my lap, and enough love in the love-tank—this remains their greatest fear—that the other twin will in some way get more.

Of course, they are essentially right. One slice of cake will always be slightly wider, one cup of juice will always be a drop fuller, one boy will always get one more minute of snuggle time, or two extra words of praise, because the world just doesn't divide neatly into equal pieces no matter how hard I try to slice and dice it.

Usually, if one triangle of apple pie comes out larger (as they tend to do), by the time I'm done attempting to equalize it, the extra bit I've added to the smaller piece ends up making the smaller portion bigger and the larger portion smaller. A twin mother is doomed to fail someone from the start.

When Quinn and Aidan begin issuing their countless demands (which began straight out of the womb in the form of tiny howls and morphed into complete sentences which now at age nine sound a bit like this: *I need water! Where's my Giants cap? Who took my shoes? Make him stop! I need new sneakers! I wanna to watch a movie! There's dog hair on my shirt! Whaddya mean dinner's not ready? What've you been doin' all day?),* sometimes I retort, "Gimme me a break, guys – I'm not an octopus!"

I have a brand new appreciation for bitches, goats, rabbits and, really, all female creatures fated to birth more than one offspring at a time. Although, I will say that having four arms or eight nipples would have helped a great deal.

The fact remains that, for twins, life will always be inherently unjust, because they burst into this crazy world together: first one, then the other, each with the same needs, demands, and desires as singletons. While parents of singletons tend to think that rearing one baby is hard, parents of multiples (or at least this one) feel generally superior, superhuman, and secretly envious of these mortals.

As extraordinary, thrilling, and cool the whole 'twin' thing is (and yes, for at least six minutes a day it's a love-fest)—it is also inherently unfair, exhausting, and maddening. Human beings were born with only one set of arms and one set of legs, and in truth there is only so much a middle-aged, over-educated, over-therapized, over-achieving twin mother can do.

It's 7:00 p.m. and dinner is an hour late. This means double meltdowns, a harried bedtime, less sleep, and another day of eternal crankiness for all of us. Add to that the fact that I'm single now (going on five years) because as nice as it was to have an extra set of arms around, I also brazenly thought it would be easier to do it myself rather than deal with an extra grumbler, who always needed a kick start and a list.

In some ways, I was right. Divorce eliminated the adult fighting, the snoring in the bedroom, and the extra clutter in the garage. But I am now constantly outnumbered by people smaller than myself, which usually feels akin to herding gophers. True, I was blessed with two boys, which the Asian women who pass me on the street tell me is *so lucky!* But according to the white ladies at the knitting store it also means I am doubly screwed. "Twin boys?" said one graying knitter with purple glasses taking in my voluminous belly, "Have a drink!"

Aidan is leaning his lanky body across the dining room table, past the Buddha sculpture that is supposed to remind everyone to be calm and kind, ha, ha, ha. He has grabbed the spoon from Quinn's hand, and if history has anything to say about it, an all-out wrestling match is about to ensue. I'm in the kitchen attempting to take the kale chips out of the oven so that my boys might ingest something green. For once in my life I'd like to sit down and eat at the same time as my children – like they do on T.V. – rather than rushing around like a maidservant fetching forgotten forks, spoons, cheese graters, and napkins.

Inevitably, each time I sit my tired ass down, someone will ask me to get something, and by the time I'm finished fetching it (just as I'm lifting the fork to my mouth), another request will come hurtling toward me like a heat-seeking-missile. This would explain why I'm constantly starving, cranky, on-the-verge-of-fainting, and how I lost all the baby weight.

Some days, I'm tempted to ask my sons, "Are your legs broken?" That's the kind of sarcastic quip my older sister would have issued. She has a live-in maid, two nannies, and a powerhouse of a career that lands her in the glamour pages of glossy magazines. I don't want to sound envious or materialistic or ungrateful, so I try to recall that there was a time when I feared I'd never be able to have kids. It's just that sometimes the insults, the dishwashing pile-up, the peanut butter on the ceiling, and the early deafness make it hard to recall what made me think that children would complete me.

Sometimes I sigh loudly like one of those mother-martyrs and I cave. "Because you said please, yes, I will get you a spoon." If it's the third time I've gotten up, I may say, "Can you get it yourself? Mama's eating now."

There's enough ravioli in the bowl for everyone to have at least six scoops, because I used the "family sized" packet, but the boys are so fearful that the other might get more that their logical brains are not working. Perhaps it's just that twinship causes a competition even more intense than ordinary sibling rivalry, because there is no oldest or youngest to establish a natural pecking order.

They are nine now. I've reminded them 101 times that they are allowed only two scoops at a time, because if I don't place this reasonable scoop limit, each one would attack the bowl like Neanderthals. Because I'm reasonable, if they empty their bowls, they are allowed seconds.

Some days, I'm astounded by my own patience, given that I was raised by a woman with the temperament of Attila the Hun. ("You will eat every piece of liver and like it!")

Often, I wish there were witnesses to my patience, because it goes without saying that whenever anyone is within earshot, that's when I end up cursing, burning my most useful finger, or shouting some permanently damaging phrase like, "What's wrong with you?" which later gets thrown back at me again and again, "What's wrong with you? What's wrong with you? What's wrong with you?" an echo to remind me of another maternal failure.

I wonder when and if this epic battle over *more* will end. In high school (if they both turn out to be straight, as I suspect they will, due to current preferences for public burping, ice hockey, and team-logo sportswear), I imagine they will compete over who gets the girl, or who gets the bigger trophy. Who gets married first? Who gets the biggest house? The coolest car? The fattest paycheck? Who keeps his hair? Who can walk without a cane? Or, if I succeed in teaching them right, maybe they'll compete over who wins the Nobel Peace Prize first? Who ends world hunger? Who stops global warming?

It's clear that my boys love and depend upon one another as fiercely as if their lungs and hearts were sewn together. They are incapable of buying a pair of sneakers without the other's approval. Neither can taste new foods without checking with his twin's taste buds, "Do you like it? Will I like it?"

I'll never forget the neonatal nurse I encountered when I was trying to swaddle my two-day-old preemies inexpertly as they lay beneath a row of heat lamps in little plastic boxes. The boys' skin was sallow, jaundiced from arriving too early into the world.

The thin-faced woman swooped Quinn out of my arms and wrapped him with the efficiency and frigidity of a factory worker wrapping a carburetor. "Twins," she muttered, "I'm a twin."

I wanted her to tell me I was going to be fine; they were going to be fine.

"My parents always bought us one gift. Every holiday. Every birthday. We never got anything that was just ours." She was middle-aged, carrying around that bitterness like an oversized suitcase.

Nine years later, I can't remember when the boys' first teeth came in, when they started eating solids, how many months it was when they took their first steps. But I remember the resentment of this woman, as if it had pinned itself to my heart. I was determined not to repeat the mistakes of her parents, or the mistakes of my mother, who set my sister and me against each other like trained pit bulls. At my grandmother's funeral, my mother wrapped her arm tightly around my sister; they walked five feet in front of me, as if I belonged to another family.

My twins would always receive separate gifts, unless it was too expensive. Or I'd make them share when it was large enough, like a train set or when it required two players, like a football. I bought them matching sweaters, or matching sweaters in different colors, so they could be equal, but separate. I labeled their water bottles with different colored rubber bands. I bought two stuffed bunnies, two matching blue raincoats with firemen and fire dogs on them, two Thomas the Choo Choo Trains, two silver lunch tins, two, two, two, and two, until our house was filled to bursting. Often I got it wrong; sometimes I got it right.

One day their paternal grandparents returned from Germany with a tiny box that rattled when you shook it. They announced, "We've brought a present all the way from Germany!" The boys jumped around like puppies in their red and blue silk Chinese pants. They searched behind their grandparents' backs for a second invisible box. My jaw tightened.

One tiny wood marionette emerged from the single cardboard box. The boys' grandparents were children of the Depression and World War II. They were careful with their money. They meant well. But I was angry that my husband had not told them after three years of present-giving that my sons were separate individuals with separate needs. I was angry that it was I who would have to field the oncoming hurricanes.

Quinn and Aidan both grabbed at the small wooden arms and pulled. I threw myself in between them to prevent one from hitting or biting, as they did back then before their words became weapons.

"You can each have a turn." I held the puppet up out of reach. "Quinn will have five minutes and then Aidan gets five."

I twisted the green kitchen timer. The ticking began. I held Quinn while he howled, "Mine! Mine! Mine!" I had to keep Aidan's tiny fist from grabbing the doll during Quinn's turn. The grandparents and the husband stood and watched.

Today, there's not a day that goes by when I'm not playing peacemaker, teaching negotiation skills, slicing fruit into equal parts, measuring out juice, then comparing the two glasses with a microscope to make sure the levels are equal.

The boys still fight over whose ball it is, who gets the last oatmeal raisin cookie, whose chair is whose, who is taller, who can throw farther, who earned more kindness marbles, whose best friend is whose. They fight over the Harry Potter LEGO set, dividing the Hogwarts castle into separate rooms, separate figures, and separate miniature swords. When I say, "This is ridiculous! Why don't you share?" they say, "Mama, it's our present. We get to decide!"

They fight over the memory of who walked first, who talked first, and Quinn even claims that Aidan is taller because he stole all the food in utero. Buried in the subtext of this conversation is the accusation, "You love him more."

Each of the boys at some point has wished death and disappearance on his brother, sometimes out loud and sometimes through the hairy eyeball stare they've perfected. My mother never hid her preferences: first for me, later for my sister. The favorite child carries the burden of guilt. The un-favored child carries the weight of feeling inadequate.

I get it now, how easily one might pick favorites. Quinn is more like me, with his hot-headed rebellious temperament, his extroversion, and his humor (although people say he looks "just like his father"). Aidan, who looks like me, is intellectual and ambitious like me, but quiet and calm like his father. I might favor them when they remind me of myself and reject them when they differ – but like any good parent, I quell these narcissistic impulses.

The boys picked their favorites early on: Quinn says he loves me more; Aidan says he loves Papa more. But I know Aidan loves me when he leans up against me while I am reading. He loves me when I introduce him to *The Odyssey* or when I take him to the art store and tell him about Picasso. Quinn loves his dad most when he lets him wrestle on the floor, or when he takes him on the stomach-flipping roller coaster, or plays hard rock. Each of us gets our turn. Erma Bombeck once wrote,

"My favorite child is the one who was too sick to eat ice cream at his birthday party – who had measles at Christmas – who wore leg braces to bed because he toed in – who had a fever in the middle of the night, the asthma attack, the child in my arms at the emergency ward."

I sit down in between the boys and say, "Remember your problem-solving tools?"

Aidan says, "When you take three scoops of ravioli *I feel* like you're being greedy!"

"Name-calling and blaming is not an 'I' statement," I explain.

Quinn howls and climbs onto the table.

"Get down!" I shriek. I cajole him into using my script. He rewrites it to craft his own verbal arrows.

"Stop interrupting!" I feel a hot flash coming on.

Finally, each boy begrudgingly says, "Next time I will take my turn first, ask Mama for help, tell on you, and only take two scoops." They roll their eyes, bump fists and say, "We get it Mama. This is soooooo dumb."

Sometimes, if I get really mad I say, "You guys are separated for 30 minutes! Go to your rooms now!"

Then it gets really, really quiet. When I go upstairs I'll find them snuggled up under Aidan's bunk bed, hiding beneath the British flag from Aidan's country-in-a-can report. Aidan is saying, "Okay, you can read *The Last Padawan* if I can read your *Avengers* book. Okay?" Quinn says, "Okay, but only if you put a bookmark in my spot." The puppy is sprawled out in between them, four little dirt-blackened bare feet sticking up from beneath the blanket and two boys reading side by side with guilty grins on their faces.

Pamela Alma Weymouth is a freelance writer, who teaches creative non-fiction and humor writing. She earned her MFA in creative writing at the University of San Francisco, after attempting to become a teacher, a social worker, an actress, and a flamenco dancer. She lives in Mill Valley with her twin boys, four hens, two mutts and an epic amount of mud, footprints, dog hair and detritus.

JOURNAL IT

What are the greatest challenges of parenting multiples at this age?

How have your multiples changed since the toddler years?

THE TWEEN YEARS

TWEEN TIPS AND ADVICE

MEGAN WOOLSEY

There are many parents and experts offering tips and advice for raising multiples in the infant and toddler stage of life when the physical labor is in full force; sleeping through the night, bottle or breast feeding, potty training, tantrums, and so much more. However, there isn't much information for parents of tween multiples. The ages between eight and 12 years old present more social and emotional challenges, for which most parents are not equipped and have no knowledge of.

During the tween years, multiples face unique challenges in school and sports. "During the tween years, there is heightened attention given to academic and athletic skills. Parents work hard not to compare the twins as the children themselves are well aware of their differences. Having someone there constantly to monitor and measure your skills can be damaging and painful. The family's challenge is celebrating individuality in the face of unrealistic societal and cultural expectations about twin connections," says Dr. Joan A. Friedman, psychotherapist and mother of twins.

Developing friendships can be unique for twins and triplets. Friedman says that issues arise for multiples in the tween years because their social skills have been stymied by their twin/triplet connection. "Either they are too comfortable having one another and therefore don't want to or are frightened to branch out and connect with other children. Or perhaps at a later age they will want to make new friendships but will feel disloyal to their twin sibling," says Dr. Friedman.

Friends of twins or triplets can feel intimidation in their relationship. "What I remember as most problematic for my kids at the tween age was making friends. Many children seemed intimidated by them. They did not develop individual friendships so friends felt they had to invite all of them over for play dates," says *Multiples Illuminated* contributor and mother of triplets, Eileen C. Manion. If friends feel they must invite all the twins or triplets to the play date, often they won't want to plan a play date with any of them. This creates a situation where they are left out of fun activities like birthday parties or other social gatherings. As parents of multiples, it is up to us to educate the public that it's okay for twins and triplets to have individual and unique experiences. Multiples learn early on that life is not always equal and fair.

SIX tips to help encourage individuality for your tween multiples:

1. Separate classes in school.

2. Separate play dates.

3. Encourage separate after-school sports and activities (which is challenging for parents, but important for multiples).

4. Refrain from intentionally or inadvertently labeling.

   - Good twin/bad twin

   - Academic twin/sporty twin

   - Extroverted twin/introverted twin

5. Pay close attention to mental health issues, especially anxiety. Multiples can have a heightened sense of anxiety for the welfare of each other.

6. If your multiples have a close relationship, do respect their need and desire to do things together.

Let's not forget to talk about the big 'P' word – puberty. Multiples will probably go through puberty at different times, because after all, they are different people. This is especially true in fraternal twin relationships where the growth rate is likely to be different during puberty. It's important to validate the smaller child—especially in middle school—when size is more visible.

The tween years are notoriously some of the most challenging years of child rearing. Raising twin and triplet tweens doesn't have to be harder than it is with singletons, but it may present different challenges. Pay close attention to your tweens' friendships and interpersonal relationships to make sure they are feeling valued and supported.

LEARNING CURVE

EILEEN C. MANION

Right after my three daughters, Deirdre, Maeve, and Kiera, were born, while I was still in The Royal Victoria Hospital in Montreal, a friend gave me a copy of Beatrix Potter's *Tom Kitten.* The opening description of Tom's mother as "an anxious parent" grabbed my attention. Will I be like that?

At first I didn't think so. But as soon as my daughters emerged from their six weeks in neonatal intensive care, I started worrying about toilet training.

During the girls' first year, everyone I talked to assured me that no child reaches adolescence in diapers.

How easy it is to minimize the hardships of the past! Some days when I pass the diaper aisle in the drugstore, I still feel smug – no more diapers for me.

Nonetheless, with potty training, I now realize I did everything wrong.

First, the babies were born in December, so they were two years old in the middle of winter, a bad time to start when everyone has to wear so many clothes.

Second, I received too much good advice. The pediatrician offered me his stock answer: "Toilet training? No problem. Just let the child come into the bathroom with you and they'll want to imitate what you do." I could see him remembering I had three. He laughed, imagining perhaps the absurdities of putting on a performance each morning. "Well, I hope you don't get constipated."

Then I consulted Doctor Spock, who advised me to watch for the child's signs of interest. The crucial thing was to identify the child's ideal point of readiness; parents should not rush things, nor should they delay too long. The ideal point of readiness might occur any time between 18 months and three years. Each child is different. Buy a potty, he suggested, when the child is about a year and a half, leave it around, available for the child to play with.

When the girls were 18 months old, I bought three potties. They showed as much interest in them as they did in any new object. They dragged the potties around their playroom, put toys into them, took toys out of them, took the potties apart, screamed until I put them back together.

Of course, they were as delighted to follow me into the bathroom as anywhere else and watched all my activities there with amazement, as they scrutinized anything else I did, whether it was folding laundry or scrambling eggs. Never in my life had I received such rapt attention for quotidian routines.

But the girls showed no sign that they'd ever use the potties for anything but block repositories or doll enclosures. Whenever I talked to friends who had successfully trained their children, I tried to delve into the mysteries. None confessed to the slightest difficulty; for all of them it had been the simplest thing in the world and they couldn't understand why I was obsessing over the issue. My friend Suzanne told me that her sister-in-law trained her daughter Emma at their summer cabin in one July day of persistent effort. "You just have to stick to it. All day." Another friend, Heather, said she'd had no trouble at all with her daughter, Jesse. When she was two and a half, Jesse got the idea sorted out during a sleep-over weekend with a five-year-old friend.

Such stories filled me with despair. I considered inviting Suzanne's sister-in-law for a visit or hiring a five-year-old consultant. I began to suspect that some kind of amnesia afflicts parents once they've dispensed with diapers; they don't remember the frustrations afterwards.

At the end of my wits, I finally asked my mother. She claimed that I'd been trained by the time I was a year old. "Why'd you put it off so long?" Was it possible that with all my fretting, I'd missed the ideal point of readiness? Was it already too late?

For the girls' second birthday, my mom sent them a book, *Joshua and the Potty*. They loved the book; they 'read' it until it fell apart, delighting in a careful examination of Joshua's penis and in enthusiastic repetition of the words "pee" and "poop." But they didn't seem to connect Joshua's bathroom adventures with anything that was happening in their own lives.

I designated the summer when they were two and a half as the ideal time for toilet training. They could run around diaper-less during vacation and make a run for the potties strategically placed near the bathroom.

Nothing worked as planned. If I suggested sitting on the lovely, familiar potty, they screamed with fear. Whenever they needed to pee or poop, they demanded a diaper, where such bodily products belonged. I returned from the holiday convinced that I'd missed Doctor Spock's ideal point and my children would never learn to use the toilet.

For their third birthday, my mother sent several pairs of Donald Duck undies. They were so intrigued that they wanted to try them on immediately. A few weeks of accidents, near misses, and occasional successes ensued. Nothing happened quickly or easily; we had no one-day or one-weekend miracles. I washed tons of extra laundry, but by Christmas they'd given up diapers entirely. I hastily gave away the half bag of Pampers I had left, to forestall any temptation to regress.

I could summarize my experience into a list of recommendations for anyone expecting twins, triplets, quadruplets, or even just one child:

1. Be sure to have the child or children in summer;

2. Don't read any advice manuals, how-to books, articles or blogs on toilet training;

3. Don't ask friends, parents, or doctors for advice. Remember that all parents succumb to amnesia after the process is over and will describe it in deceptively simple terms – as I probably have;

4. Keep in mind that no matter how bad your experience is, you, too, will forget the whole thing afterwards, as completely as will your child.

Could I apply these life lessons to other areas of conflict? The next big hurdle was teaching the triplets to read.

At first it had seemed odd that my friend gave me a book while I was still recovering from my emergency C-section and the babies were in rectangular plastic boxes, either very dozy or sleeping.

But as soon as I got them home, I realized he was prescient. Apart from feeding and diapering, what can you do all day with babies? Read to them – why not? I started with poetry, then progressed to narrative.

I can't remember a time when they didn't love books – handling them, looking at them, chewing on them. We went through several copies of *Green Eggs and Ham*, as well as *The Cremation of Sam McGee*, two big favorites.

Both their dad and I are college teachers who learned to read before starting school. Since my daughters adored books and having parents, babysitters, friends, or anyone else read to them, I thought teaching them to read would be easy.

But when you're an anxious parent, nothing is easy.

At five, my daughters still loved being read to but showed no interest in taking on the task themselves. Since we were still living in Montreal, we thought it would be a good idea for them to learn French, so they went to French immersion kindergarten. They picked up speaking a second language quickly, but reading remained something adults did for them.

In first grade, they finally learned to read – in French. Books in their first language, however, remained opaque. Isn't reading a transferrable skill?

In second grade, they were required to do a research project. I took them to the library, helped them find appropriate books (pre-internet era) – all in French. English still seemed to be the language in which adults read, not children.

As with potty training, summer seemed the ideal time to focus on the project. So, we designated the summer between second and third grade for the big push on reading. We were planning to move to the U.S. for three years, so the girls would be required to read in their mother tongue, we told them.

I didn't read anything on the subject. Why should I? I'd been reading for most of my life and teaching since I was an adult.

I tried to avoid asking for advice or making invidious comparisons, but it seemed like everyone I talked to had their kids reading by age three. Were my children alone destined to illiteracy?

At first, there was fierce resistance to reading even the easiest preschool books. We had to enforce 30 minutes of reading per day while on vacation. They didn't want to fail third grade, did they? Everyone else would be reading chapter books and they couldn't even manage a picture book?

Reading, which had been such an unmitigated pleasure for the girls when their parents did it for them, began to seem onerous, something they had to do before going to the beach or the park – like eating your Brussels sprouts before getting dessert. Had I completely spoiled it for them?

I was almost in despair when some friends came to stay for a few days with their six-year-old son. He brought along a copy of *Stay Out of the Basement* – one of the early Goosebumps books.

Maybe he discussed it with the girls or he told them something about the book that intrigued them. From one day to the next, it seemed, the atmosphere shifted.

No longer did we need to impose the 30-minute required reading time. Soon it was more like, "Put the book away for now. It's time for lunch."

I'll be forever grateful to R.L. Stine for writing books that were intriguing enough to break through whatever barrier was keeping the triplets from reading. Subsequently, they grew up with Harry Potter, and when their dad declined to read it, Maeve, in a dramatic role reversal, read the whole series to him.

Will we forget those tense interactions?

The other day I asked Maeve what she remembered about learning to read.

"It was hard," she replied immediately.

For me, reading seemed analogous to eating. I'd been so proud of my homemade baby food – not a morsel of Gerber's passed their lips.

But one day Maeve pushed away the spoon. She wanted to do it herself. The other two immediately imitated her, but they all lacked the hand-eye-mouth coordination for cutlery. Would they starve?

They neither died from malnutrition nor flunked third grade.

I'd like to think the reading phase will fade into the foggy past as did eating and potty training – one more chapter in the uneasy struggle of renouncing dependence on their side and ceding control on mine.

Eileen C. Manion grew up in New York and moved to Montreal in 1969 where she got her Ph.D. in English at McGill University. Since the mid-1970s, she has been teaching English at Dawson College in Montreal. In 1987, she had triplet daughters, one of whom currently lives in Canada, while the other two are in the U.S.

THE SIX-WORD MEMOIR

KRISTEN WILLIAMS

My son Jonah came up to me one day and said, "Ma, for English class we have to write a six-word memoir, and I don't know what to write."

I blurted out, "I am not my twin brother." We both laughed; the twins are mirror-image identical, but I don't think they look identical one bit. Then again, I am their mother. In the beginning, when they were aware enough to realize that most people couldn't tell them apart, it didn't bother them. Now they're approaching the teenage years, and they're hitting that stage of development where this can make or break them. And I'm doing my best to make sure that they know their worth both as individuals and as twins.

I've never been one to dress them identically; similarly, sometimes, but never the same. I was very conscious of wanting to treat them as two separate individuals. They've always been dressed (and have dressed themselves) differently.

Now that they're 12 going on 13, they are definitely two distinct individuals who happen to closely resemble one another. Jonah is introverted, more likely to stay home and practice his violin or stick his nose in his tablet; Eli is extroverted and friendly, the president of the student body, and often hangs out with friends. They're brothers who bicker and argue and make each other laugh like no one else can; two separate individuals with opposite personalities, interests, and temperaments. Twins who, as I write this, are separated by distance (with Eli staying with my mother for the weekend) but are both on the computer, playing the same game with each other and Facetiming so they can still talk.

In other words, they're what both my husband and I wanted when we found out we were having twins: a unit comprised of two different people.

Sometimes, Jonah gets pulled aside by teachers and asked if he can stay after class to help with set-up for some school function; he politely waits for the teacher to finish speaking before calmly saying, "I'm Jonah, not Eli." The teacher is always embarrassed, but we've told both of them that this is going to happen since they look so similar. People usually think Jonah is Eli; Eli is rarely mistaken for Jonah. I don't know why; maybe because Eli is so involved in school, volunteering his time and being the loud, extroverted, social creature he is (much like his mother). Jonah is more content to be quiet and let Eli take the lead (much like his father).

I asked Jonah if it bothers him that people often mistake him for his brother.

"Not really," he told me. "Sometimes, maybe." Then he gave me his "oh well" half-smile and shrugged. As his mother, my heart aches; I wish I could give him whatever it is that Eli and I both have, that thing that makes it easy for us to just dive into any situation and make our presences felt. That thing that makes it easy for us to go up to strangers and ask for the things we want.

That thing that makes people know who we are.

I know I gave him those things the moment he was conceived. I've raised the twins the same; all of my boys have been treated with the same regard, so I know that one twin's extroversion and the other's introversion are genetic, inherent; nothing I can change, so I don't try. I simply offer him my hand and a hug and ask him if there's anything I can do to make him feel better, if, in fact, he wants to feel better.

Sometimes he says yes, sometimes no; he always takes the hug, though.

He's also my funny child. They're all hilarious, but Jonah has this biting, quick wit that is never cruel, while Eli's humor is very warm and infectious. Both twins have dimples but on opposite cheeks – Eli's right cheek dimple is deep and cute and impossible to resist. Jonah's is more a parenthesis creasing his left side, smarmy and smirky, punctuating whatever weisenheimer thing he's just said.

They look most alike right after a haircut, which is going to happen soon. Right now, they resemble Wolverine when they wake up, cowlicks in the back poofing on either side of their head. They'll get their haircuts, and it'll start up again.

"I'm Jonah!" he'll wail. Mostly jokingly. Grandmothers, teachers, friends. When the twins get haircuts, no one can distinguish between the two.

When I blurted out to Jonah that his memoir should be "I am not my twin brother," I was joking and said it unthinkingly, sticking my hand out and counting off the words until I reached the first finger on my other hand. But in that moment when Jonah laughed and tilted his head to the side, his left cheek creasing deeply as he smirked (and let's face it, chided me), our eyes met and I saw the slight sadness there. Because we both knew it was something that sometimes bothers him, being mistaken for his twin.

But then, in true Jonah style, he rolled his eyes and laughed it off.

Because it will happen again and again, and we both know it.

I'm proud of my kids for not being angry about it, or resentful. I don't know what I did, whether it was something I said to them or some bit of DNA I passed along, if anything. I don't know why my kids have such easy, affable humors and temperaments, but I'll take it.

And I'll be glad when they aren't resentful when they get their haircuts and people mix them up.

Including me.

Yes, me.

I've been known to not be able to tell them apart from behind when they get their haircuts.

The look of mock betrayal in whose-ever eyes of baleful brown cuts me deep every time.

"I'm *Eli*!" or

"I'm *Jonah*!"

"God, Mom, don't you know your own children?" hollers the other twin from wherever he's located.

Ah, well. I'm only human.

Kristen Williams is a novelist who occasionally picks up work staffing conventions for fun and to get out of the house. She enjoys meeting people from all over the world, crafting her feelings, liquid matte lipstick, and cooking without recipes.

INDIVIDUALITY, MUTUALITY, AND A GAME OF TWISTER

ANDREA LANI

Left foot yellow. Right hand blue. Right foot blue. Left hand red. Left hand green. Left foot yellow again.

We are playing *Twister* on a Tuesday night, my idea to keep everyone from disappearing to their personal screens after dinner. I, as usual, have been assigned spinner and judge duties, and 11-year-old twins Emmet and Zephyr are on the mat. They are uniquely suited to this game. They're both flexible to the point of being double-jointed. They're tall enough to just barely reach across the mat, but short enough that their center of gravity is low. They both play aggressively, aiming for the farthest dots in an attempt to stymie their opponents, usually knocking their taller and less bendy dad and big brother out early in the game.

Right now, their arms and legs are stretched to their fullest extent, their butts are hovering inches off the floor, and their limbs are woven together in an impenetrable knot. This is another thing that gives them an advantage in *Twister*—having been in close physical contact since they were a single egg, they are comfortable with the kind of breakdown in personal-space boundaries the game engenders, in ways most of us aren't. Sprawled across the mat, limbs entwined, with their matching (for the first time ever) hair styles of growing-out buzz cuts and similar facial features, they look a bit like a two-headed, many-limbed beast.

That is one of the drawbacks of being twins; people tend to see them as a single entity, a two-headed creature. Zephyr recently lamented, "Everyone treats us like the same person!" and people often ask me whether the boys have different personalities. It's kind of a silly question, because of course they do. How could two separate people have the same personality? But it's complicated, because they are more similar to each other in many ways than, say, two singleton siblings or two close friends. Yet their differences, while sometimes subtle, are present and ever-changing. Adult friends and relatives try to categorize them: the outgoing one, the energetic one, the quiet one, the athletic one. Not only are these categorizations usually inaccurate, they're reductive. No one's personality can be boiled down to a single character trait. Each day, or moment, one aspect of our personality may come to the fore, but most of us are not being continually compared to another person the way twins are.

Psychologists theorize that when infants are born they don't recognize themselves as independent from their mothers; they must go through a process of separation and individuation to develop their own identities. It's thought that twins also have a sense of oneness with each other at birth and must separate not only from their mother but also from their twin in order to develop unique identities.

When Emmet and Zephyr were very small, I read twin parenting manuals that recommended parents help along the individuation process by actively providing each twin his own space and activities—separate bedrooms, wardrobes, and toys; time alone with each parent; different classrooms and extracurricular activities. But I've always found that these recommendations are based on an assumption of resources—time, money, space, energy—which is unrealistic for many, if not most, families. We live in a small house with only two bedrooms, the second of which is shared by the twins and their older brother. Emmet and Zephyr started out in a shared bed—first a co-sleeper, then a crib, then a mattress on the floor, which their older brother moved into for a time—because of space and finances and it was easier when I was taking one baby after the other in and out of bed all night. When their brother was ready for his own bed, we built bunk beds with a double-sized bottom bunk which the twins shared for a few more years, until Zephyr moved to the futon in our sunroom and we realized it was time to build him his own loft bed.

My children attend a small school, where opportunities for separate classrooms and different after-school activities are limited. I always dressed Emmet and Zephyr differently, but from the same pool of clothes. And as working parents, we've rarely had the luxury of time to spend alone with individual children, preferring to engage in family activities that include all of us. In short, we did almost nothing to promote separateness between our sons as recommended by the parenting experts whose books I read.

But I'm not too worried that I've burdened my sons with the 'twin mystique' and an over-reliance on each other, being of the mind that if I provide my children with a supportive, loving environment, with plenty of opportunities to explore and try new things, and encouragement to pursue their interests, they will grow into their own best selves, with little interference on my part. Identical twin and anthropologist Dona Davis, in an article entitled 'How Twin Culture Challenges Our Notions of Self,' seems to agree. She takes issue with the ways that parents are encouraged to promote individuation in twins. "The scientific literature … is dominated by Western egocentric notions of the self," she writes. "The view that the self is a private, bounded, unique center of awareness—a one that stands in contrast to others—is taken for granted. Twin researchers fail to see how that view is formed by culture and history; indeed, the socially constructed nature of it goes wholly unrecognized and unexamined." (Davis, 2016)

Davis contends that modern psychology and psychiatry pathologize twinness, regarding the twin bond as an unhealthy relationship that needs to be cured. Davis sees twins in a different light. "Identical twins," she writes, "actually have a more finely developed awareness of their uniqueness than do singletons, and this understanding goes beyond physical features. Identical twins personify a kind of enhanced self. Having an identical twin does not compromise one's self at all—instead, each twin enriches both the self and the other. Twindividuals do not see independence and mutuality as opposites or as having a zero-sum relationship to one another." (Davis, 2016)

Mutual means shared, reciprocal. In our culture, which tends to idealize the individual and mythologize self-reliance, mutuality can be suspect. But twins can teach us much about caring for and relying on each other while maintaining our own uniqueness. My sons' relationship flows back and forth between intense closeness and independence without the friction and anxiety that characterizes even close friendships and marriages. They are equally comfortable entangled in a game of Twister as they are off playing alone.

As if to prove Davis's point, Emmet and Zephyr went through their most profound period of individuation this past summer, when the five of us spent two months in almost constant close contact with each other. As a family, we drove from Maine to Colorado, spent a week with relatives, visiting and acclimating, then hiked together from Denver to Durango on the 500-mile Colorado Trail. Each day for six weeks, we all ate the same food, hiked the same stretch of trail, slept in the same nine-by-nine tent. We depended on each other and had to work together as a unit to make our miles and complete the necessary camp chores. The only alone time anyone got was when we hiked at different paces, stretched out along the trail. Our personal possessions were pared down to the bare minimum, and each person was responsible for carrying, packing, and taking care of their own belongings. For the first time in their lives, Emmet and Zephyr each had his own distinct items, from sleeping bag to t-shirt, backpack to pocket knife.

Amid all of this intense time together, each boy's unique character traits came through. Emmet's infinite capacity for discomfort—inside-out-backward clothes, shoes on the wrong feet, granola bar wrappers stuffed down inside rain pants worn on a hot day, backpack diagonal across his back—kept him moving down the trail with nary a complaint. Zephyr's sharp eyes spied hawks on the wing, bighorn sheep on top of mountain peaks, and, once, a weasel catching and killing a pika. Emmet, who hated our camp food more than anyone and loved the few incidences of trail magic we enjoyed, bought candy to hand out to other hikers. Zephyr got up early to take pictures of the sunrise. Emmet carried a book on the outside of his pack and sat down to read at every rest break. Zephyr made plans for Thanksgiving dinner and a farm store he wants to run when he grows up. Emmet thought of better ways to manage everything, from hiking trails to motels to restaurants to health insurance. Zephyr picked tiny wild strawberries as he hiked, giving half of his harvest to me. Emmet was the only one of us to climb to the top of Cony Summit, a 13,334-foot mountain whose peak the trail skirted past (and he piled up rocks to add five feet to the mountain's height while he was up there). Zephyr encouraged me up switchbacks to saddles with cries of, "Nearly there!" Emmet sang a made-up song about the benefits of rain while we huddled beneath our umbrellas, cold, tired, and hungry, waiting out a downpour.

Davis writes, "Mutuality comes from shared experience and leads to a sense of togetherness, but does not imply any diminishment of identity or individuality." Not only did the shared experience of hiking 500 miles together not diminish Emmet and Zephyr's individuality, it allowed each boy's unique identity to flourish. After we returned home, their process of individuation continued—they played independently, biked alone to the neighborhood general store, went to friends' houses separately. We crossed a big milestone when they asked to have separate clothing and drawers and we spent a day sorting their clothes into two piles, which they each folded and placed into one half of their shared dresser. The clothes still look the same to me—t-shirts and athletic pants—but each boy knows what is his.

Right foot green. Left hand blue. Right foot yellow.

Zephyr lunges for the farthest dot on the mat and, in the process, upsets the precarious balance he and Emmet had achieved as a two-headed creature. They collapse on the floor in a tangle of limbs and laughter. They will beg to play again, entangling and collapsing over and over. They might let their dad and brother in on the action for a few rounds. Then they will head off to dress in their different pajamas, drawn from their own drawers, crawl into their separate beds, and dream their individual dreams.

In 2016 Andrea Lani left a 17-year career as an environmental regulator to hike across Colorado with her husband and three sons and write a book about that adventure, a similar hike 20 years earlier, and two decades of change in the Rocky Mountains. Her writing has appeared in Snowy Egret, Saltfront, *and* Brain, Child Magazine, *among others, and she's an editor at* Literary Mama. *She lives with her family in Maine.*

JOURNAL IT

What do you look most forward to as your multiples head into their teen years?

How would you describe your multiples' relationships with each other right now?

THE PERFECT PARENT

MEIMEI FOX

Remember,
at the start of this roller coaster ride,
when you were just imagining these beings into life,
when they were no more than a flame tended carefully in
your heart,
how you thought it would be?

Fabulous fun!
Swimming in a sea of giggles.
Melting into smiles and cooing that could
vanish snow on an icy day.
A love so powerful, like you'd never known –
putting another life before yours.
Dedicating all that you have and all that you are
to raising these precious, magnificent souls.

And of course, you,
in your immense love and wisdom:
The Perfect Parent.

Well …

Some of your dreams have come true.
Yes, yes, you do-

Have the laughter, the bonding, the joy,
the LOVE
that threatens to swallow you whole.
It's all there.

And so is the struggle.
So are the moments of crisis and self-doubt.
So are the times you wonder what it's all about.

Like the time when—
You leave the room for five seconds and return to find
three children covered in sunscreen, head to toe,
screaming as it drips into their eyes.

The time when—
You discover a box stacked precariously on top of a chair,
one child toppling a houseplant
while the other tears its leaves into little pieces.

The time when—
A temper tantrum happens.
In the middle of the grocery store. Or the doctor's office. Or
on the plane.
And other people start shooting you dirty looks like,
"Why can't you control your child?"

The time when—
you all get the stomach flu at the same time.
Disgusting fluids coating every surface of your home.
Four days of misery.
Ten loads of laundry.
When the only parenting happening is being done by an
iPad.

The time when—
Your children first scream at you,
"I hate you!"
When you just have to breathe, and do your best not to
react, and
know that they don't really mean it.
They love you,
they just don't love how you're telling them, "No."

And yet …
In spite of all these challenges,
all the tough times,
You wouldn't change a single thing.

Other people may give a bit of a smirk when they see you
strolling by with twins (or more):
"Double trouble!" they say.
"Double happiness," you reply, grinning with pride.

Because life surrounds you.
It may threaten to engulf you at times, but it is *here*,
like fireflies dancing across the summer sky.
And it is, truly, a miracle!

Over time, you learn to laugh at the Mommy Wars.
The next time another parent tells you that you should try this or
buy that product or
do such-and-such better or
really, you shouldn't ever let your child say or do *that* …
You just give a warm smile and say, simply, "Thanks."

You burn your copy of *How to Raise the Perfect Child*,
which has been sitting on your bedside for the past 12
months or years
leaving you with nothing more than the gnawing feeling
that
you aren't enough.

You put your phone away.

And you sit down on the floor to play LEGOs and dolls
with your children for an hour.
You get muddy building a fort in the yard.
You go to soccer practice, and actually watch the game
instead of Facebook.
You feel your heart burst when they stand before you, all
dressed up for school photos, looking like little adults for the
first time.
You dance across the living room with a tiny hand squeezed
tightly in yours.
You feel your eyes moisten when one kid hears the other
crying,
and rushes to hand her a favorite toy.
You even smile when they throw their pasta onto the ground
and
yank each other's hair.

Because this is it.
This is all there is.
This is all that matters.
This is all that counts.

Not the dos and the don'ts,
not the shoulds and the shouldn'ts,
or the times you let technology take over because you were
just too tired.

144

Not the achievements or classes or comparisons,
or meltdowns in the grocery aisle,
or scoldings that were too strict,
or boundaries that were not held tightly enough.

Not the numerous mistakes you, your partner, and your
children are sure to make.
Only this.

Being together. Being present.
Showing up with heart and forgiveness.

What being a parent of multiples teaches you is that
if you do just that,
you're already doing *more than enough.*

The only thing that matters in this precious life
is love.

And all you have to do to be "the perfect parent"
is pay attention.

MeiMei Fox is a New York Times bestselling author who regularly blogs for The Huffington Post and MindBodyGreen, among other publications. Also, MeiMei works as a life coach, assisting clients in realizing their most ambitious dreams. She graduated Phi Beta Kappa with honors and distinction from Stanford University, with a BA and MA in psychology. MeiMei lives in Hawaii with the Love of Her Life, her husband Kiran Ramchandran, and their twin boys. Her mantra is Fear Less, Love More! MeiMei writes about raising and traveling with twins in her blog, Adventures with Twins.

HELPFUL TIPS FOR SURVIVING AND THRIVING DURING THE TODDLER TO TWEEN YEARS

EDITORS AND CONTRIBUTORS

When someone offers to babysit, take them up on it. Even if it's so that you can go to the store by yourself for an hour. Or seven.

- Kristen Williams

The expression "choose your battles" will never have as much meaning as it does when you are staring down the face of a toddler on the verge of eruption. While it is important to follow through on consequences, keep in mind what matters. You are the only person who will care if your child's clothes don't match (or if he/she is wearing the same shirt over and over). Saying yes to the small things makes them more receptive when you say no to the big ones.

- Caryn Berardi

My biggest tip is to start practicing holding hands and walking places as soon as you can; realizing I could ditch the giant stroller and keep everyone together safely was a magical moment. The second tip would be to remember that although it may not feel like it now, even the most gray hair-inducing episodes will be great stories some day!

- Emily Lindblad

Snacks. All the time. You don't want to be outnumbered by the hungry.

- Jared Bond

Pay attention to mental health issues, especially anxiety. Multiples may have a heightened anxiety about one another and their welfare.

- Eileen C. Manion

Potty training twins don't always have to be done at the same time. Sometimes it's okay to spread the joy out over time. When they start school, accept that you can't be two places at once and there will be times when you let one of them down. They start not loving dressing alike between five and seven, so get it out of your system. Puberty does not hit at the same time, so be prepared for this joy also to be spread out over time. And be brave. Know you can take them places like the pool or a museum or an airport and keep them safe. Know they can still be close even if you decide to keep them separate at school. Know that there will be times when you have to console one who is incredibly disappointed while you have to cheer for the other who succeeded. But be brave, because you can do it.

- Whitney Fleming

Build a routine from wake-up to bedtime that you stick to 99.9% of the time. After each event or outing, restock, pack, lay out (whatever it may be) for the next day. Clothes, pajamas, on-the-go snacks in the diaper bag. Prepping intermittently throughout the day for the next alleviates some of the pain and energy that goes into getting out of the house, which unto itself is an unpredictable feat.

- Jessica Martineau

Though it may be difficult, set aside alone time for each child. It teaches them that you value them as individuals and it allows them their own time to feel important and special. You will enjoy the one-on-one dynamic and the (momentary) peace of not being outnumbered.

- Shanna Silva

Don't forget to laugh. The worst experiences make the best stories!

- MeiMei Fox

There is no point in buying multiples of the same thing for your twins or triplets. They'll just fight over one and discard the other. I found that when we designated items as belonging to a specific child, they lay claim to their own only. That applies to toys, cutlery, water bottles, and even their spots at the dining table. No more fighting!

- Alison Lee

Keep in mind the big picture. Something that may be an insurmountable problem today (potty training, sleep issues, even behavioral challenges) will not be a problem a year from now.

- Amy Kestenbaum

Don't compare yourself to other moms. Why? Because moms lie. I suffered from self-doubt and worry until I figured this out. No mom can live up to impossible standards—or be happy every minute, or never lose their patience—but many pretend they do. Give your best effort, love your kids, and know that you're doing an awesome job, Mom.

- Maureen Bonatch

Follow the Boy Scout Motto and Be Prepared! This is how I make it through everything, from bath time to carting a group of little ones around when I have to drop big ones at events and activities. We have a backpack diaper bag that is stocked with books, paper, crayons, pencils. It stays packed and ready to go. I include hand sanitizer and snacks as needed. Finally, DumDum lollipops and a digital device such as a Kindle have gotten me through some tricky times.

- Rebecca Borger

Divide and conquer. Or just divide. If you had to share your room, your friends, your toys, and your genes with another person, you'd get sick of him, too. When bickering ensues, gently (or loudly) encourage your multiples to find some space where they can be alone and get a break from each other.

- Andrea Lani

I'm a twin, and here's my tip. During your multiples' toddler to tween years, their relationships to each other are still forming and growing. Don't force them together or apart, but let their relationships form naturally, and stop all comparisons in their tracks.

- Kari Lutes

Try to cultivate empathy in your children. They will learn it by watching you and modeling your behavior. If they're able to experience the feelings of others, your kids will grow into compassionate, ethical, and secure adults.

- Shelley Stolaroff Segal

When your kids are battling over "Who got more?": 1. Validate the feeling. 2. Establish the rule. 3. Establish expected behavior. 4. Praise and reward positive behavior. I try to avoid food and material rewards which lead to food/shopping addictions, and materialism. Instead I offer non-material privileges when possible. Example: Validate: I know you're hungry. 2. Rule: Everyone gets two scoops of ravioli to start. 3. Establish expected behavior: Quinn I see you sitting quietly so you may go first. 4. Praise and reward.

- Pamela Alma Weymouth

Kids always think everything needs to be fair. This is especially true for multiples, since they are moving through life at the same age. When one of my triplets thinks they should get to do or have something just because their sibling did, we talk about how life can still be fair even if things aren't always equal. Fair does not mean equal; it means everyone is getting what they need.

- Megan Woolsey

Tuck away the fact that the part of a multiple's brain that says, "THIS IS A BAD IDEA," is often canceled out by a former wombmate urging," YOU SHOULD TOTALLY DO THAT, IT'S HILARIOUS!"

- Jackie Pick

Discourage competition and labels. There is so much external pressure to define which is the smart one or the strong one or the funny one; resist that. When you tell them you love them, tell them something about them that makes them special to you.

- Gina Granter

Get used to people asking you if you are dressing them as Thing 1 and Thing 2 for Halloween.

- Briton Underwood

ACKNOWLEDGEMENTS

I would like to thank my partner in this book writing, editing and publishing adventure, Alison, who is truly a gift. Alison, I can always count on you to come through and I have learned so much from watching and listening to your life and writing wisdom. Over the years, we have built a beautiful friendship.

To my husband, Chris, who continues to be an invaluable support system for me. Chris, you always push me to go out there and follow my dreams. Your loyalty to our family is unwavering.

Ava, Elsa, Violet and Preston. . . if I didn't have you, who knows where or who I would be right now. I often wonder if I would be a writer and publisher at all if it weren't for you. Who would've thought that triplets and their big sister would even allow for any time to follow my dreams, but life works in indescribable ways. I hope you don't hate me one day for sharing stories of your upbringing with the whole world. I hope you feel proud, because each of you are all energy and love, and I can't wait to see what you do with your gifts.

I want to give a special and warm thanks to my parents, Jim and Sally Traub and my in-laws, Richard and Sherri Woolsey, who provide incredible support to us as we raise our big family. You can always be counted on to come to our rescue when we need help, or come babysit when we want to have a much-needed getaway. I hope you know how loved and appreciated you are.

AWKNOWLEDGEMENTS

Thank you to the 19 talented contributors who lent your stories to make this book something truly special that we can all be proud of. Thanks to our foreword writer, Dr. Joan A. Friedman, for offering *Multiples Illuminated* your expertise and writing a riveting story to begin our book. We appreciate all your support!

To my Motherland. These are difficult times with a divided country and contentious politics. I will never give up fighting to make this country fair and equal to all, because that is who we are meant to be. #shepersisted.

~ Megan

Putting a book together is a Herculean task, and in my case, I know I could not have done this alone. Thanks to my amazing partner, Megan, I didn't have to. You're the best! I still marvel at the fact that despite our distance, we pulled this off.

Putting a book together is also time-consuming, and I think I spent hundreds of hours working on it, which would not have been possible if it was not for my husband who picked up the slack and told me to shut the door to work in peace. Thank you, my partner in life. I love you.

My four children, always my inspiration, thank you for your daily shenanigans which keep my head out of the clouds, and my feet on the ground. I love you all with every fiber of my being.

My sister Sharlene and my best friend Deviga – I love you both! Life without you would be dull and less bright, and I'm glad I don't have to know what that's like.

Thank you to our foreword writer, Dr. Joan A. Friedman, for being a friend and supporter to *Multiples Illuminated* from day one. We are honored to have your words in our book. A big thank you to our blurb writers, beta readers, friends, fans, and contributors to the book and our website: we could not possibly do this without you.

Last but not least, thank you to my dear friends: Arnebya, Angie, Angela A., Angela Y., Anna, Andrea, Brittany, Debi, Elaine, Erin, Greta, Jennifer, Kate, Keely, Kiran, Kim, Kirsten, Kristin, Laura, Leigh Ann, Poppy, Sarah, Tracy, Tonya, and Val. Thank you for being you, and being there for me. I love you all.

~ Alison

ABOUT THE EDITORS

Megan Woolsey is a writer living in California with her supportive husband, a set of triplets, and their big sister. Megan is published in many national publications including *Cosmopolitan*, *Good Housekeeping*, The Huffington Post, BonBon Break, Scary Mommy, Parent.co, and more. She is an essayist in two anthologies. For a list of her work, go to MeganWoolsey.com.

Alison Lee is an editor, writer, and entrepreneur. Her writing has been widely featured on various websites such as Mamalode, On Parenting at The Washington Post, The Huffington Post, Everyday Family, Scary Mommy, BonBon Break, Parent.co, Brain, Child Magazine, Feminine Collective, and Mothers Always Write. She is a contributor to two anthologies, *My Other Ex: Women's True Stories of Leaving and Losing Friends* and *So Glad They Told Me: Women Get Real About Motherhood*. Alison lives in Malaysia with her husband, two boys and boy/girl twins. Find out more at AlisonSWLee.com.

Multiples Illuminated was founded by Megan Woolsey and Alison Lee, both writers and mothers of multiples (triplets and twins respectively). Together, we birthed our first anthology, *Multiples Illuminated: A Collection of Stories and Advice From Parents With Twins, Triplets and More*, featuring essays from 20 talented writers and parents of multiples. These essays tell stories of struggles with infertility, the journey with IVF and surrogacy, the struggles and triumphs of pregnancy, labor and delivery, the trials and tribulations in the NICU, and the amazing first years with multiples.

Multiples parents have a special and unique bond that tie us together. Our hope is that readers will find value and entertainment connecting with fellow parents and learning about their journey.

**Have you read the first book in the
Multiples Illuminated series?**

MULTIPLES ILLUMINATED:
A COLLECTION OF STORIES AND ADVICE FROM PARENTS
OF TWINS, TRIPLETS, AND MORE

Did you just discover that you are pregnant with twins, triplets or more? Are you wondering how you will cope caring for more than one baby?

Multiples Illuminated: A Collection of Stories and Advice from Parents of Twins, Triplets and More dives deep into the world of raising multiples with beautiful stories and helpful advice. In it, you will find essays on infertility help and hope; finding out and coping with a multiples pregnancy; stories of labor and delivery and the NICU; breast feeding best practices for multiples; and surviving the infant and toddler stages.

Purchase now from Amazon:
https://www.amazon.com/Multiples-Illuminated-Collection-Stories-Triplets/dp/0996833501

This is an excerpt of an essay **Two for One** *by Becki Melchione. To read more stories like this, please check out the book* **Multiples Illuminated: A Collection of Stories and Advice from Parents of Twins, Triplets and More,** *available in paperback and e-book format.*

My husband Luc and I knew that there was a chance of twins before we were pregnant. We created that possibility by transferring two embryos instead of one. The decision came after a tangled path of cancer and infertility during which we were forced to reevaluate every notion of motherhood we held. At that pivotal moment, when asked what we wanted to do, we looked at each other without question. "Two," we said simultaneously. "Let's transfer two embryos." Two increased our odds of having one baby. That's all we wanted.

Months of research and conversations around cancer and fertility produced no black and white choices, only the murkiness of unenviable statistics. Every step led to a compromise between hope and fear. The type of cancer I had, a melanoma of the eye, was albino rare. The majority of those diagnosed with it were members of AARP, not the PTA. Survival rates were projected over 20 years, a steady decline into the single digits. In 20 years, I would be 54.

Certain melanomas were known to be estrogen sensitive. That gave my oncologist pause. Dr. Pink had treated a woman in her early 30s, like me, whose melanoma spread in a hormone-fueled frenzy during her pregnancy. Dr. Pink's naturally relaxed demeanor turned grave. It was clear that her patient's outcome had not been good, but I couldn't ask what happened. Cancer casualty stories still spun me into a downward spiral of anxiety and worry.

"If you need someone to carry a baby for you, I'd be honored," my sister Cara had offered shortly after I began treatment. Her offer, previously stashed in the back of my mind, reemerged when Dr. Pink suggested that an alternative way to create our family would be safest.

Still, the idea of having a baby the usual way tumbled around the stubborn edges of my mind. I could do it, ignore my trusted doctor's advice, but it was an unknowable risk. Some days, I had come to terms with this. If I knew that she would have people to love her, my husband and our families, to raise her, I gladly would have given my life to bring the daughter I always imagined into the world. This way makes the world what I always imagined. It would have been one last way to say, "Screw cancer!"

Other days, I couldn't decide if it was fair to her to bring her into the world knowing that there was a significant chance of leaving her motherless. What damage would that do to a child, a teenager, a young woman? When you want something so desperately, you suddenly notice it everywhere. Soon, stories of women who grew up motherless appeared— in magazines, as a writing assignment from a fellow student, in conversations with a co-worker. Despite my fears that my daughter would be damaged forever, the universe presented the opposite. It said that she would survive and might even be stronger as a result.

But what struck me most were the memories these children of lost mothers held close: those of cooking together, decorating for holidays, perusing vacation photo albums, reading a favorite book, hugs after a tough day. "Mom" was a loving presence, not simply the woman who birthed them. That's what I wanted: to kiss her boo-boos and lay next to her reading stories that would waft her off to dreamland. I wanted to brush her hair into ponytails and braids and put funny makeup on her for Halloween. I wanted all those moments for my memories because, to her, they would be what Mom does. She wouldn't know how close she came to not having them, that they might have been Daddy kissing her hurts and Grammy braiding her hair. Having a surrogate was a gift, insurance on some level that I would be there for her.

MULTIPLES RESOURCES

Multiples of America (aka National Organization of Mothers of Twins Clubs)

The Multiples of America aka NOMOTC is a 501(c)(3) nonprofit organization dedicated to supporting families of multiple-birth children through support, education, and research. Multiples of America promotes support and networking for parents of multiples. Opportunities for self-help, emotional support and parenting information are provided through local club and state organization meetings.

Multiple Births Canada

Multiple Births Canada's mission is to improve the quality of life for multiple-birth individuals and their families in Canada. They fulfill their mission by providing support, education, research, and advocacy both nationally and internationally to individuals, families, Chapters, and organizations that have a personal or professional interest in multiple-birth issues.

Twins and Multiple Births Association (TAMBA)

Tamba – Twins and Multiple Births Association – is the UK's leading twins and triplets charity. Packed full of advice and information about what to expect while pregnant, breast feeding advice and even information about schooling, it is the only UK-wide charity working to improve the lives of twins, triplets, or more and their families.

Twins Magazine

TWINS™ Magazine is the premiere magazine for parents of multiples, from twins and triplets to quadruplets, quintuplets and more! Published six times each year, TWINS™ Magazine is the "bible of parenting multiples," loved by moms and dads of twins and higher-order multiples since 1984.

Twiniversity

Now reaching almost 100,000 families in over 150 countries, Twiniversity is the largest global resource for all things 'twinnie.' With worldwide recognition in her field, Natalie Diaz brings her twin parenting expertise to their online resource and parent-to-parent forums.

Twins Doctor

Launched in 2007, TwinsDoctor.com is the first physician-authored website to provide health information exclusively for multiples.

Babies in Belly

Babies in Belly offers convenient, virtual prenatal classes taught by a certified teacher and mother of monozygotic twin boys.

Raising Multiples

Raising Multiples was founded as MOST (Mothers of Supertwins) in 1987 by a community of families, volunteers and professionals. They are the leading national nonprofit provider of support, education and research on higher-order multiple births.

Twin Pregnancy and Beyond

Lovingly founded by a mother of twins in 2007 on the basis of offering the best and most up-to-date 'twin-specific' information and support on all aspects of twins – from finding out about your twin pregnancy, through twin birth, raising twins and beyond.

The Twin to Twin Transfusion Syndrome Foundation

The Twin to Twin Transfusion Syndrome Foundation is the first and only international nonprofit organization solely dedicated to providing immediate and lifesaving educational, emotional, and financial support to families, medical professionals and other caregivers before, during and after a diagnosis of twin to twin transfusion syndrome.

Twins Day Festival

The Twins Days Festival is the largest annual gathering of twins and multiples in the world and takes place every August in Twinsburg, Ohio. It's open to all twins and multiples, young and old.

Twins Online

A helpful and informative site loaded with topics covering all aspects of twins.

Centre for the Study of Multiple Birth

This nonprofit organization was founded in 1977 by identical twins Louis and Donald Keith to promote research, education, and public service for multiple births.

Dad's Guide to Twins

A dad's guide to all things twins, including finance, how to raise healthy babies, tips for physically caring for two, getting twins to sleep, and more.

KellyMom

This is one of the most comprehensive websites for moms, and was developed to provide evidence-based information on breast feeding and parenting. Kelly is the mother of three lovely children, and an International Board Certified Lactation Consultant (IBCLC).

New Mommy Media

Based in San Diego, New Mommy Media is a network of dynamic audio podcasts. Their shows give tips and advice for new parents, educating and entertaining moms and dads as they transition into parenthood. Each 30-minute episode features everyday parents and experts discussing relevant issues in a relaxed, roundtable format, and they have a weekly podcast called *Twin Talks*.

Joan A. Friedman, Ph.D

Dr. Friedman is a prominent and well-respected twin expert who shares her passionate views and insights about twins and their emotional needs with twins and their families throughout the world. The fact that she is an identical twin and the mother of five, including fraternal twin sons, makes her ideally suited to this task. Her commitment to twin research and her treatment of twins of all ages demonstrate the breadth and depth of her skills and experience.

Jumelle

This Canadian website run by Lynda Haddon offers information regarding multiple births. It includes pregnancy and postnatal information and, from the point of view of new parents, attempts to address some questions and concerns of multiple-birth parents.

Twinless Twins Support Group

This organization provides a safe and compassionate community for twinless twins to experience healing and understanding. They also provide support for twins and other multiples who have lost their twin due to death or estrangement at any age.

Stuff 4 Multiples

Great gear for multiples children with useful reviews of products.

Twin Multiples Club

Where having more than one baby at a time is looked upon as special and not crazy.

How Do You Do It? (HDYDI)

Moms of multiples tell it like it is.

Twin Love Concierge

A maternity consulting service exclusively for twins.

About Twins

About-twins.com wants to prepare twin parents for the task of raising two well-adjusted, independent children. They want moms and dads around the world to have loads of fun in their role as parents of twins, while still having an outlet to discuss concerns and anxiety in relation to being a twin parent.

CONNECT WITH US

Thank you for reading our book. We believe strongly in community and connecting, first and foremost, in our journeys as parents of multiples. Our experiences are unique, and often, we find it difficult to relate to families of singletons. We want to put our books into as many hands of multiples families as possible, and book reviews on Amazon, Goodreads, and other sources where books are purchased, are essential to the success of this goal. We would love for you to leave us a review when you finish this book! Thank you in advance.

Looking for a community of fellow parents of multiples? Want to contribute a story to our blog? Visit the Multiples Illuminated website: www.multiplesilluminated.com

Do you love exclusives? Then sign up for our newsletter, which we send out only once or twice a month: http://eepurl.com/bW3X0D

Any questions? Email Multiples Illuminated: multiplesilluminated@gmail.com

Love news on twins, triplets, and more? Like Multiples Illuminated on Facebook: www.facebook.com/MultiplesIlluminated

Talk to us! Tweet Multiples Illuminated on Twitter: www.twitter.com/MultiplesIllum

Pin with Multiples Illuminated on Pinterest www.pinterest.com/MultiplesIllum

10238087R00106

Printed in Germany
by Amazon Distribution
GmbH, Leipzig